Nova Latina

Book 2

R C Bass

Nova Latina Book 2

© R C Bass 2022

First published: 2022

ISBN 979 8 8399011 0 0

This printing: August 2022

Also available via Amazon:

Nova Latina Book 2 Specimen Answers ISBN
Nova Latina Book 1 ISBN 979 8 5991905 3 0
Nova Latina Book 1 Specimen Answers ISBN 979 8 7228054 2 3
Streamlined Greek ISBN 978 0 9576725 8 1
Streamlined Greek Answer Book ISBN 978 0 9576725 9 8
Prep School Greek: A workbook leading to CE Level 1 ISBN 978 0 9576725 7 4
More Prep School Greek: A workbook leading to CE Level 2 ISBN 978 1 5272261 3 5
Latin as an Honour Book 1 ISBN 978 0 9576725 0 5
Latin as an Honour Book 2 ISBN 978 0 9576725 3 6
Latin as an Honour Book 3 ISBN 978 0 9576725 4 3
Latin as an Honour Answer Book ISBN 978 0 9576725 5 0
Prep School Latin Book 1 ISBN 978 1 0897232 2 6
Prep School Latin Book 2 ISBN 978 1 6871152 0 1
Prep School Latin Book 3 ISBN 978 1 6871929 2 9
Prep School Latin Book 4 ISBN 978 1 6887813 1 3
Prep School Latin: A Handbook for Students and Teachers ISBN 978 0 9576725 6 7

Published by Galore Park:
Latin Vocabulary for Key Stage 3 ISBN 978 0 9036276 6 5
Latin Pocket Notes ISBN 978 1 9070477 1 8

Typeset by R C Bass

Celiae uxori regenitae

Contents

Introduction to the Teacher   iii

Chapter 39   The Story of Troy (Part 1)   1
Discord, the goddess of arguments, gatecrashes the wedding party of Peleus and the sea-nymph Thetis.
ceteri and -que

Chapter 40   The Story of Troy (Part 2)   3
On Mount Olympus the three goddesses Juno, Minerva and Venus argue over the golden apple.
Third declension masculine and feminine nouns (rex)

Chapter 41   The Story of Troy (Part 3)   10
Jupiter passes the buck to Paris, prince of Troy.
Third declension neuter nouns (vulnus)

Chapter 42   The Story of Troy (Part 4)   15
The goddesses cheat.
The future tense: 1st and 2nd conjugations

Chapter 43   The future tense: the other conjugations, and *to be*   18

Chapter 44   The Story of Troy (Part 5)   21
Venus wins and promises Paris Helen, wife of Menelaus of Sparta.
ubi and quamquam clauses

Chapter 45   The Story of Troy (Part 6)   23
Paris leaves Troy, goes to the Greek city of Sparta and kidnaps Menelaus' wife Helen.
Verb revision

Chapter 46   The Story of Troy (Part 7)   26
Menelaus appeals for help from other cities in Greece, and the combined Greek forces sail to Troy, where the fighting begins.
is, ea, id

Chapter 47   The Story of Troy (Part 8)   31
The Greeks realise that capturing Troy will not be a five-minute job.
The Greek warrior Achilles wants to take revenge on the Trojan Hector.
The pluperfect tense

Chapter 48   The Story of Troy (Part 9)   38
Achilles, angry because of Patroclus' death, tells Hector he will kill him.
Hector is not impressed.
Third declension adjectives in -is (fortis)

Chapter 49   The Story of Troy (Part 10)   42
Achilles fights Hector.
Third declension adjectives like audax and ingens

Chapter 50   The Story of Troy (Part 11)   46
Achilles mistreats Hector's body. Hector's brother, Paris, takes revenge.
Comparison of adjectives

Chapter 51   The Story of Troy (Part 12)   51
The Greeks despair of taking Troy, but Ulysses (Odysseus) comes up with a plan.
possum

Chapter 52   The Story of Troy (Part 13)   54
              The Trojans see the horse, but cannot decide what to do with it.
              nonne and *num*; prohibitions

Chapter 53   The Story of Troy (Part 14)   59
              The fall of Troy.
              Cardinal numbers 1-20; personal and reflexive pronouns

Reading Passages in Workbook Format   65

Reference Section   81

              List 1:   Vocabulary Checklist   82

              List 2:   Principal Parts Checklist   85

English-into-Latin Sentences Revision

              List 3a: Latin only checklist   87

              List 3b: English-Latin alphabetical   88

              List 3c: English-Latin by word-type   89

              List 3d: English-Latin word groupings   90

Grammar Reference

              List 4a: Grammatical terms   91

              List 4b: Nouns   92

              List 4c: Adjectives   94

              List 5:   Pronouns   98

              List 6:   Prepositions   100

              List 7:   Verbs   102

              List 8:   Syntax   104

              List 9:   Cardinal numbers   107

Level 1 Revision Check-list   108

Level 2 Revision Check-list   109

              List 10:   English-Latin Quick Reference   110

              List 11:   Latin-English Quick Reference   115

Introduction to the Teacher

This volume provides continuity and progression from Book 1, its grammar and vocabulary being mapped exactly to the new CE Level 2 specification, whose first summer session is that of 2023. It follows the quasi-workbook and two-way vocabulary approach of Book 1.

A pdf of this volume is available free of charge and on request via email. Colleagues should feel free to circulate these to their pupils, preferably within their own establishment only, and perhaps buy at least a single hard copy! A slim volume of specimen answers is in preparation.

I am especially grateful to Nicholas Richards, Head of Classics at Christ Church Cathedral School, Oxford, and his eagle-eyed pupils, without whose constructive nit-picking there would be even more errors in this volume than whatever remain.

R C Bass
August 2022
robertcharlesbass@gmail.com
www.rcbass.co.uk

Chapter 39: The Story of Troy (Part 1)
ceteri and *-que*

Exercise 39.1

*Discord, the goddess of arguments, gatecrashes
the wedding party of Peleus and the sea-nymph Thetis.*

1　olim in <u>monte Olympo</u> dei et deae <u>laetissimi</u> erant. cibum consumebant et vinum bibebant. <u>laetissimi</u> erant quod Peleus <u>Thetim in matrimonium ducebat</u>. Thetis dea erat. Peleus vir <u>mortalis</u> erat. dei deae<u>que</u> laeti erant. ridebant.

5　subito tamen Discordia, dea mala, intravit. <u>ceteri</u> dei, ubi Discordiam viderunt, non laeti erant. non iam ridebant. non ridebant quod Discordiam non amabant. clamaverunt:

　　'quid cupis, Discordia? cur hic stas? te non amamus. statim discede!'

10　Discordia <u>nuntiavit</u>:

　　'me audite, dei! me audite, deae! <u>donum</u> habeo. <u>donum</u> pulchrum habeo. hic est.'

　　deinde Discordia <u>pomum</u> <u>deposuit</u>. risit discessit<u>que</u>. dei deae<u>que</u> ad <u>pomum</u> <u>appropinquaverunt</u>. <u>pomum</u>
15　spectaverunt.

monte Olympo = Mount Olympus

laetissimus, -a, -um = very happy

Thetim *is the accusative of Thetis*

in matrimonium duco (3) = I marry

mortalis = mortal

-que = and (*before the word it is attached to*)

ceteri = the rest of

nuntio (1) = I announce

donum, -i n. = gift, present

pomum, -i n. = apple

deposuit = (she) put down

appropinquo (1) = I approach

(a copy of this passage in workbook format can be found on page 66.)

Exercise 39.2

1.　From the passage above, give, in Latin, an example of:

　　a. a verb in the imperfect tense;　...

　　b. a verb in the perfect tense;　...

　　c. a part of the verb *to be*;　...

　　d. an adverb;　...

　　e. an imperative.　...

2.　**Discordia** (line 8). In which case is this noun?　...

3.　**risit** (line 13). For this verb, give:

　　a. its person;　...

　　b. its number;　...

　　c. its tense;　...

　　d. the first person singular of its present tense.　...

Vocabulary Box 27a		Vocabulary Box 27b	
appropinquo, -are, -avi (1)	I approach	and	-que
ceteri, -ae, -a	the rest of	I announce	nuntio, -are, -avi (1)
(endings like the plural of *bonus*)		I approach	appropinquo, -are, -avi (1)
nuntio, -are, -avi (1)	I announce	the rest of	ceteri, -ae, -a
-que	and		(endings like the plural of *bonus*)

Notes on the vocabulary

1. ceteri, -ae, -a (endings like the plural of *bonus*) = *the rest of*

   Don't be fooled by the 'of' into thinking along the lines of a noun in the genitive case!

   The rest of the girls = ceterae puellae (NOT ceterae puellarum!)

2. -que = *and*

   et is not the only way of saying 'and' in Latin. Another way is to use the word ending -*que*, but there is an important feature to note about word order:

   -*que* at the end of a word is the same as an *et* **in front of** that word.

   So: *Boys and girls*   = pueri puellae**que**
                                = pueri **et** puellae
       He is shouting and fighting   = clamat pugnat**que**.
                                = clamat **et** pugnat.

Exercise 39.3

Translate into English:

1. Romulus Remusque pueri Romani erant.

2. puellae currebant ridebantque.

3. magister pueros puellasque monet.

4. dominus intrat servumque malum punit.

5. ceteri servi timent.

6. templum sacrum pulchrumque est.

7. deos deasque semper laudamus.

8. dominus servum malum punivit. ceteros servos laudavit.

9. servi cibum aquamque rogabant.

10. ubi Discordia intravit, ceterae deae non laetae erant.

Chapter 40: The Story of Troy (Part 2)
Third declension masculine and feminine nouns (*rex*)

Exercise 40.1

On Mount Olympus the three goddesses Juno, Minerva and Venus
argue over the golden apple.

1   dei deaeque in <u>monte</u> Olympo erant. <u>pomum</u> spectabant. <u>pomum</u>
pulchrum erat. <u>pomum</u> <u>aureum</u> erat. <u>haec</u> verba in <u>pomo</u> erant: '<u>hoc</u>
<u>pomum</u> <u>aureum</u> feminae <u>pulcherrimae</u> est.'

<u>Iuno</u> regina deorum erat. <u>et</u> <u>soror</u> <u>et</u> <u>uxor</u> <u>Iovis</u> erat. dea Iuno <u>pomum</u>
5   spectavit. verba legit.

'ego dea <u>pulcherrima</u> sum,' clamavit. '<u>pomum</u> igitur meum est.'
dea Minerva <u>pomum</u> spectavit. verba legit.

'<u>erras</u>, <u>Iuno</u>,' clamavit. '<u>pomum</u> meum est. <u>pomum</u> meum est quod
ego <u>pulcherrima</u> sum.'

10   dea Venus <u>pomum</u> spectavit. verba legit.

'<u>erratis</u>, deae. ego <u>pulcherrima</u> sum. <u>pomum</u> igitur meum est. <u>pomum</u>
<u>mihi tradite</u>!'

sic <u>tres</u> deae de <u>pomo</u> <u>aureo</u> <u>disputabant</u>. <u>omnes</u> <u>pomum</u> habere
cupiebant. ad <u>Iovem</u> appropinquare igitur constituerunt. <u>Iuppiter</u> <u>et</u>
15   <u>pater</u> <u>et</u> <u>rex</u> deorum erat.

mons, montis m. = mountain	
pomum, -i n. = apple	
aureus, -a, -um = golden	
haec = these	
hoc = this	
pulcherrimus, -a, -um = the most beautiful	
Iuno = Juno	
et... et... = both... and...	
soror = sister	
uxor = wife	
Iuppiter, Iovis m. = Jupiter	
erro, -are, -avi (1) = I am wrong	
mihi tradite! = hand over to me!	
tres = three	
disputo, -are, -avi (1) = I argue	
omnes = (they) all	
pater = father	
rex = king	

(a copy of this passage in workbook format can be found on page 67.)

Exercise 40.2

1.   From the passage above, give, in Latin, an example of:

a. an imperative;

....

b. an infinitive.

....

2.   **pomo** (line 2).

a. In which case is this noun?

....

b. Why is this case used?

....

3.   **deorum** (line 4).

a. Give the case of this noun.

....

b. Give the gender of this noun.

....

4.   **erat** (line 4). For this verb, give:

a. its person;

....

b. its number;

....

c. its tense;

....

d. the first person singular of its present tense.

....

Vocabulary Box 28a		Vocabulary Box 28b	
mater, matris f.	mother	mother	mater, matris f.
pater, patris m.	father	father	pater, patris m.
frater, fratris m.	brother	brother	frater, fratris m.
soror, sororis f.	sister	sister	soror, sororis f.
parens, parentis m./f.	parent	parent	parens, parentis m./f.
rex, regis m.	king	king	rex, regis m.
uxor, uxoris f.	wife	wife	uxor, uxoris f.
mons, montis m.	mountain	mountain	mons, montis m.
et … et …	both … and …	both … and …	et … et …
erro, -are, -avi (1)	I am wrong; I wander	I am wrong, wander	erro, -are, -avi (1)
trado, -ere, tradidi (3)	I hand over	I hand over	trado, -ere, tradidi (3)

Third declension nouns: masculine and feminine group

This is the largest declension (noun group) in Latin. There are two kinds of third declension nouns: masculine/feminine ones; and neuter ones. We're going to deal with the masculine/feminine group first.

In dictionaries and wordlists you will find four pieces of information about third declension nouns, set out like this example:

rex, regis m. king

1   2   3   4

1   The first word is the nominative and vocative singular.
2   The second word, ending in **-is**, is the genitive singular.
     *If you remove this **-is** you will be left with the all-important **stem**. The importance of this will be seen shortly.*
3   This letter indicates the gender: masculine, feminine or neuter.
4   This is the English meaning.

The way to work out the various parts of third declension masculine/feminine nouns is summarised in this table:

	singular	plural
nominative	(given in wordlist)	stem + **es**
vocative	(same as above)	stem + **es**
accusative	stem + **em**	stem + **es**
genitive	stem + **is**	stem + **um**
dative	stem + **i**	stem + **ibus**
ablative	stem + **e**	stem + **ibus**

Applying this to the sample noun *rex, regis* results in the table on the next page:

	singular	plural
nominative	rex	reg**es**
vocative	rex	reg**es**
accusative	reg**em**	reg**es**
genitive	reg**is**	reg**um**
dative	reg**i**	reg**ibus**
ablative	reg**e**	reg**ibus**

Now practise chanting through all the endings of the third declension nouns of Vocabulary Box 28, on the opposite page.

Handy Reminder before diving into Exercise 40.3 below!

Remember that the **stem** of a third declension noun is the genitive singular of that noun with the **-is** removed!

Exercise 40.3

Give the:

1. accusative plural of *pater, patris* m., father ....

2. genitive singular of *uxor, uxoris* f., wife ....

3. dative plural of *mons, montis* m., mountain ....

4. ablative singular of *mater, matris* f., mother ....

5. genitive plural of *soror, sororis* f., sister ....

6. dative singular of *pater, patris* m., father ....

7. ablative plural of *uxor, uxoris* f., wife ....

8. accusative singular of *soror, sororis* f., sister ....

9. accusative singular of *pater, patris* m., father ....

10. vocative singular of *rex, regis* m., king ....

5

Exercise 40.4

Give the:

1. genitive singular of *rex, regis* m., king ....

2. nominative singular of *uxor, uxoris* f., wife ....

3. dative singular of *mater, matris* f., mother ....

4. vocative singular of *pater, patris* m., father ....

5. dative plural of *frater, fratris* m., brother ....

6. accusative singular of *mons, montis m., mountain* ....

7. ablative singular of *soror, sororis* f., sister ....

8. accusative plural of *mater, matris* f., mother ....

9. ablative plural of *frater, fratris* m., brother ....

10. genitive plural of *pater, patris* m., father ....

Handy Help

	singular	plural
nominative	(given in wordlist)	stem + **es**
vocative	(same as above)	stem + **es**
accusative	stem + **em**	stem + **es**
genitive	stem + **is**	stem + **um**
dative	stem + **i**	stem + **ibus**
ablative	stem + **e**	stem + **ibus**

Exercise 40.5

Give the:

1. dative singular of *frater, fratris* m., brother   ....

2. nominative singular of *pater, patris* m., father   ....

3. vocative singular of *mater, matris* f., mother   ....

4. vocative plural of *frater, fratris* m., brother   ....

5. dative singular of *soror, sororis* f., sister   ....

6. accusative singular of *parens, parentis* m./f., parent   ....

7. ablative singular of *rex, regis* m., king   ....

8. accusative singular of *uxor, uxoris f., wife*   ....

9. ablative plural of *mons, montis m., mountain*   ....

10. genitive plural of *parens, parentis* m./f., parent   ....

Handy Help

	singular	plural
nominative	(given in wordlist)	stem + **es**
vocative	(same as above)	stem + **es**
accusative	stem + **em**	stem + **es**
genitive	stem + **is**	stem + **um**
dative	stem + **i**	stem + **ibus**
ablative	stem + **e**	stem + **ibus**

Exercise 40.6

Translate into Latin (your answer must be a single Latin word):

1. by the mountains   ....

2. to the sister   ....

3. brothers! (vocative)   ....

4. of the wives   ....

5. for the wife   ....

6. sister (object)   ....

7. mothers (object)   ....

8. to the fathers   ....

9. for the parents   ....

10. mothers (subject)   ....

Handy Help

brother	frater, fratris m.
father	pater, patris m.
king	rex, regis m.
mother	mater, matris f.
mountain	mons, montis m.
parent	parens, parentis m./f.
sister	soror, sororis f.
wife	uxor, uxoris f.

	singular	plural
nominative	(given in wordlist)	stem + **es**
vocative	(same as above)	stem + **es**
accusative	stem + **em**	stem + **es**
genitive	stem + **is**	stem + **um**
dative	stem + **i**	stem + **ibus**
ablative	stem + **e**	stem + **ibus**

Exercise 40.7

Translate into English:

1. montem vidi.
2. pater currit.
3. uxorem meam amo.
4. rex regit.
5. matrem amamus.
6. fratrem et sororem habeo.
7. rex sororem pulchram habet.
8. multos montes vidimus.
9. montem altum spectamus.
10. uxor mea iam venit.

Exercise 40.8

Translate into English:

1. Iuppiter rex deorum erat.
2. Iuno erat et uxor et soror Iovis.
3. puella cibum patri parabat.
4. puer sororem non amat.
5. servi ad montem festinaverunt.
6. non sunt multae viae in montibus.
7. rex matrem patremque amabat.
8. dominus uxorem pulchram habet.
9. patrem bonum habeo.
10. soror mea mala est.

Exercise 40.9

Translate into English:

1. puer cum sorore semper pugnat.
2. puella cum fratre semper pugnat.
3. pater pueri iratus est.
4. rex terram bene regit.
5. vir pecuniam sorori dat.
6. puella pecuniam regis capit.
7. mater mea fratrem clarum habet.
8. frater matris meae clarus est.
9. puer multa dona matri dedit.
10. uxor regis pulchra est.

Exercise 40.10

Translate into Latin:

1. I warned my parents.
2. I used to have a sister.
3. We feared the king.
4. He killed his sister.
5. We loved our mother.
6. You (sg) saw the mountains.
7. He loved his wife.
8. They saw the mountain.
9. She had a brother.
10. The brothers and sisters were running.

Exercise 40.11

Translate into Latin:

1. I have a beautiful wife.
2. The king had many wives.
3. My mother's garden is beautiful.
4. Mountains are high.
5. My parents are famous.

Exercise 40.12

Translate into Latin:

1. The king killed his own parents.
2. He has both a brother and a sister.
3. The boys were playing with their mothers.
4. The prisoners fought against the king.
5. We often give gifts to our parents.

Chapter 41: The Story of Troy (Part 3)
Third declension neuter nouns (*vulnus*)

Exercise 41.1

Jupiter passes the buck to Paris, prince of Troy.

1   tres deae, ubi ad Iovem venerunt, haec verba dixerunt:

'Iuppiter, pomum aureum nos tres deae cupimus. quis est pulcherrima? lege! lege nunc!'

Iuppiter non laetus erat. iram dearum timebat.

5   'deae,' respondit, 'vos omnes pulcherrimae estis. vos omnes corpora pulcherrima habetis. ego legere non possum. est iuvenis, Paris nomine. in urbe Troia habitat. feminas pulchras amat. Paris pulcherrimam leget. Paridem rogate!'

tres deae iratae erant. Paridem tamen rogare constituerunt. itaque
10   ad Paridem ierunt. iter non longum erat. mox igitur ad Paridem advenerunt. Paris, ubi lucem claram in caelo vidit, timebat. deae Paridem salutaverunt et omnia de pomo aureo narraverunt.

'Iuppiter nos ad te misit, Paris. te deam pulcherrimam legere iubet. lege nunc!'

tres = three
Iuppiter, Iovis m. = Jupiter
haec = these
pomum, -i n. = apple
aureus, -a, -um = golden
pulcherrimus, -a, -um = the most beautiful
nunc = now
omnes = all
corpora = bodies
possum = I am able, I can
iuvenis, iuvenis m. = young man
nomine = by name
urbs, urbis f. = city
leget = (he) will chose
Paris, Paridis m. = Paris
ierunt = (they) went
iter, itineris n. = journey
longus, -a, -um = long
advenio, -ire, -veni (4) = I arrive
lux, lucis f. = light
saluto, -are, -avi (1) = I greet
omnia = everything
narro, -are, -avi (1) = I tell

(a copy of this passage in workbook format can be found on page 68.)

Exercise 41.2

1. From the passage above, give, in Latin, an example of:

   a. a preposition;

   b. an imperative;   ....

   c. an infinitive;   ....

   d. an adjective.   ....

   ....

2. **dixerunt** (line 1). For this verb, give:

   a. its tense;

   b. the first person singular of its present tense.   ....

3. **deae** (line 5). In which case is this noun?   ....

   ....

4. **habetis** (line 6). For this verb, give:

   a. its person;

   b. its number;   ....

   c. its tense.   ....

   ....

Vocabulary Box 29a	
iuvenis, iuvenis m.	young man
lux, lucis f.	light
urbs, urbis f.	city
corpus, corporis n.	body
flumen, fluminis n.	river
iter, itineris n.	journey
mare, maris n.	sea
nomen, nominis n.	name
vulnus, vulneris n.	wound
advenio, -ire, -veni, -ventum (4)	I arrive
narro, -are, -avi (1)	I tell
saluto, -are, -avi (1)	I greet
longus, -a, -um	long
nunc	now

Vocabulary Box 29b	
city	urbs, urbis f.
light	lux, lucis f.
young man	iuvenis, iuvenis m.
body	corpus, corporis n.
journey	iter, itineris n.
name	nomen, nominis n.
river	flumen, fluminis n.
sea	mare, maris n.
wound	vulnus, vulneris n.
I arrive	advenio, -ire, -veni, -ventum (4)
I greet	saluto, -are, -avi (1)
I tell	narro, -are, -avi (1)
long	longus, -a, -um
now	nunc

Third declension nouns: neuter group

This is the same as masculine/feminine nouns like *rex, regis,* only different!

In dictionaries and wordlists you will, again, find four pieces of information given:

vulnus, vulneris n. wound

1   2   3   4

1   The first word is the nominative, vocative **and** accusative singular.
2   The second word, ending in **-is**, is the genitive singular.
    *If you remove this **-is** you will be left with the all-important **stem**. The importance of this will be seen, again, shortly.*
3   This letter indicates the gender: neuter.
4   This is the English meaning.

The way to work out the various parts of third declension neuter nouns is summarised in this table:

	singular	plural
nominative	(given in wordlist)	stem + **a**
vocative	(same as above)	stem + **a**
accusative	(same as above)	stem + **a**
genitive	stem + **is**	stem + **um**
dative	stem + **i**	stem + **ibus**
ablative	stem + **e**	stem + **ibus**

Note that the nominative, vocative and neuter plurals here end in -a. If you remember your table of *bellum,* you will not be surprised to learn that these are the usual endings for all neuter nouns.

By using the example of *vulnus, vulneris* n. wound (so the stem = *vulner-*) and applying these rules, we get:

	singular	plural
nominative	vulnus	vulner**a**
vocative	vulnus	vulner**a**
accusative	vulnus	vulner**a**
genitive	vulner**is**	vulner**um**
dative	vulner**i**	vulner**ibus**
ablative	vulner**e**	vulner**ibus**

Now practise chanting through the endings of the third declension neuter nouns of Vocabulary Box 29 on the previous page.

Note the following table of *mare, maris,* n. sea, which is a bit of a one-off. It differs from the table of *opus* in the ablative singular and the nominative, vocative and accusative plural.

	singular	plural
nominative	mare	mar**ia**
vocative	mare	mar**ia**
accusative	mare	mar**ia**
genitive	mar**is**	*(does not exist!)*
dative	mar**i**	mar**ibus**
ablative	mar**i**	mar**ibus**

Exercise 41.3

Give the:

1. nominative plural of *nomen, nominis n.,* name

2. accusative singular of *iter, itineris n.,* journey

3. genitive singular of *corpus, corporis n.,* body

4. ablative plural of *flumen, fluminis n.,* river

5. dative plural of *mare, maris n.,* sea

6. dative singular of *iter, itineris n.,* journey

7. ablative singular of *nomen, nominis n.,* name

8. accusative plural of *corpus, corporis n.,* body

9. nominative singular of *mare, maris n.,* sea

10. vocative singular of *flumen, fluminis n.,* river

Exercise 41.4

Translate into Latin:

1. by name

2. names (object)

3. bodies (subject)

4. to the river

5. the sea (object)

6. for the journey

7. of the rivers

8. of the sea

9. for the journey

10. by rivers

Handy Vocabulary

body	corpus, corporis n.	river	flumen, fluminis n.
journey	iter, itineris n.	sea	mare, maris n.
name	nomen, nominis n.		

Exercise 41.5

Translate into English:

1. nauta mare non timet.

   ....

2. iter longum sed pulchrum erat.

   ....

3. liberti corpus portabant.

   ....

4. multa itinera longa fecimus.

   ....

5. aqua fluminis alta erat.

   ....

6. sunt in urbe multa templa.

   ....

7. oppida et urbes non amo.

   ....

8. nomen regis Romulus erat.

   ....

9. pater meus trans mare solus saepe navigat.

   ....

10. amici itinere fessi erant.

    ....

Exercise 41.6

Translate into Latin:

1. The mother was afraid of the river.

   ....

2. The king was making a long journey.

   ....

3. On the journey we saw many young men.

   ....

4. The sea does not frighten sailors.

   ....

5. The woman had a beautiful body.

   ....

Exercise 41.7

Translate into English:

1. multa corpora in proelio vidi.
2. iter iuvenum et longum et miserum erat.
3. rex lucem claram in caelo vidit.
4. nomen urbis Roma erat.
5. puellae iuvenes pulchros saepe salutant.
6. pater magnam pecuniam iuveni dedit.
7. matrem patremque in urbe heri vidi.
8. corpus nautae magnum erat.
9. ad flumen mox venimus.
10. itinere fessi, mox dormivimus.

Exercise 41.8

Translate into Latin:

1. The boy was standing in the river.
2. The name of the young man was Marcus.
3. We saw the rivers and the sea.
4. The waves of the sea were big.
5. Mother does not like long journeys.

Exercise 41.9

Translate into English:

1. mater bona est.
2. regem bonum laudo.
3. fratremne habes?
4. captivus diu currebat.
5. magister cucurrit.

Exercise 41.10

Translate into English:

1. iuvenes advenerunt.
2. urbes spectamus.
3. vina bibebamus.
4. cur corpora portatis?
5. lucem vidimus.

Exercise 41.11

Translate into English:

1. flumina longa sunt.
2. urbem diu oppugnabatis.
3. dona accipere amamus.
4. pueri montes viderunt.
5. poeta librum scribebat.

Exercise 41.12

Translate into English:

1. iuvenis currit.
2. iter longum facimus.
3. iam advenio.
4. rex urbem cepit.
5. urbs pulchra erat.

Chapter 42: The Story of Troy (Part 4)
The future tense: 1st and 2nd conjugations

Exercise 42.1

The goddesses cheat.

1 Paris timebat. respondit tamen: 'omnes pulcherrimae estis, deae! nunc legere non possum. cras redite! cras constituam!'

deae Paridi 'cras redibimus,' clamaverunt, 'sed diu exspectare non cupimus.' iratae discesserunt.

5 secreto tamen Iuno ad Paridem appropinquavit. haec verba Paridi dixit:

'si mihi pomum trades, ego te virum potentissimum faciam.' postquam haec verba dixit, discessit.

Minerva quoque ad Paridem secreto appropinquavit. haec verba
10 Paridi dixit:

'si tu me leges, ego te virum sapientissimum faciam.' postquam haec verba dixit, discessit.

postea Venus quoque ad Paridem secreto appropinquavit. haec verba Paridi dixit:

15 'si tu me leges, ego tibi feminam pulcherrimam uxorem dabo.' deinde discessit.

Paris solus iam erat.

Paris, Paridis m. = Paris	
omnes = all	
pulcherrimus, -a, -um = very beautiful	
possum = I am able, I can	
cras = tomorrow	
redibimus = we will come back	
exspecto, -are, -avi (1) = I wait (for)	
secreto = in secret	
Iuno = Juno	
haec = these	
si = if	
pomum, -i n. = apple	
mihi = to me	
potentissimus, -a, -um = the most powerful	
faciam = I shall make	
postquam = after	
sapientissimus, -a, -um = the wisest	
postea = later	
uxorem = as your wife	
dabo = I shall give	
solus = alone	

(a copy of this passage in workbook format can be found on page 69.)

Exercise 42.2

1. From the passage above, give, in Latin, an example of:

   a. an infinitive; ....

   b. an imperative; ....

   c. a personal pronoun; ....

   d. a preposition. ....

2. **dixit** (line 10). For this verb, give:

   a. its person; ....

   b. its number; ....

   c. its tense; ....

   d. the first person singular of its present tense. ....

3. **Paridem** (line 13).

   a. In which case is this noun? ....

   b. Why is this case used? ....

	Vocabulary Box 30a		Vocabulary Box 30b	
cras	tomorrow	after	postquam
exspecto, -are, -avi (1)	I wait (for)	alone	solus, -a, -um
heri	yesterday	later	postea
hodie	today	today	hodie
postea	later	tomorrow	cras
postquam	after	I wait (for)	exspecto, -are, -avi (1)
solus, -a, -um	alone	yesterday	heri

The future tense: 1st and 2nd conjugations

The future tense indicates an action which will take place in the future – no surprise there. The key English words here are *will* and *shall*. Here are the endings for *amo*-type and *moneo*-type verbs. The endings are identical, but note the underlined vowel linking the stem to the ending:

	1 *love*	2 *warn*
I shall	am**a**bo	mon**e**bo
You (sg) will	am**a**bis	mon**e**bis
He/She/It will	am**a**bit	mon**e**bit
We shall	am**a**bimus	mon**e**bimus
You (pl) will	am**a**bitis	mon**e**bitis
They will	am**a**bunt	mon**e**bunt

Exercise 42.3

Translate into English:

1. aedificabunt.
2. iubebo
3. respondebitis.
4. stabunt.
5. salutabimus.
6. oppugnabunt.
7. clamabit.
8. terrebitis.
9. delebunt.
10. dabitis.

Exercise 42.4

Translate into Latin:

1. We shall stand.
2. They will carry.
3. I shall destroy.
4. He will have.
5. We shall approach.
6. You (sg) will hold.
7. I shall overcome.
8. They will welcome.
9. We shall call.
10. She will fight.

Exercise 42.5

Translate into English:

1. appropinquabimus.   ....

2. delebit.   ....

3. manebo.   ....

4. rogabo.   ....

5. ridebimus.   ....

6. videbo.   ....

7. movebunt.   ....

8. stabit.   ....

9. monebitis.   ....

10. habitabunt.   ....

Exercise 42.6

Translate into Latin:

1. I shall answer.   ....

2. You (sg) will see.   ....

3. They will overcome.   ....

4. She will laugh.   ....

5. You (pl) will sail.   ....

Chapter 43
The future tense: the other conjugations, and *to be*

	3 *rule*	3½ *take*	4 *hear*	irregular *be*
I shall	reg**am**	cap**i**am	aud**i**am	ero
You (sg) will	reg**es**	cap**i**es	aud**i**es	eris
He/She/It will	reg**et**	cap**i**et	aud**i**et	erit
We shall	reg**emus**	cap**i**emus	aud**i**emus	erimus
You (pl) will	reg**etis**	cap**i**etis	aud**i**etis	eritis
They will	reg**ent**	cap**i**ent	aud**i**ent	erunt

Exercise 43.1

Translate into English:

1. regemus.
2. legam.
3. advenietis.
4. curram.
5. trades.
6. constituemus.
7. eris.
8. fugiam.
9. mittent.
10. cupietis.

Exercise 43.2

Translate into Latin:

1. He will eat.
2. They will be.
3. We shall drink.
4. We shall run.
5. He will send.
6. We shall play.
7. You (pl) will decide.
8. You (sg) will read.
9. They will play.
10. I shall depart.

Handy Vocabulary

advenio (4)	I arrive	I am	sum (irreg)
bibo (3)	I drink	I arrive	advenio (4)
constituo (3)	I decide	be	sum (irreg)
consumo (3)	I eat	I decide	constituo (3)
cupio (3½)	I want	I depart	discedo (3)
discedo (3)	I depart	I drink	bibo (3)
fugio (3½)	I flee	I eat	consumo (3)
lego (3)	I read	I flee	fugio (3½)
ludo (3)	I play	I hand over	trado (3)
mitto (3)	I send	I play	ludo (3)
rego (3)	I rule	I read	lego (3)
sum (irreg)	I am	I rule	rego (3)
trado (3)	I hand over	I send	mitto (3)
		I want	cupio (3½)

Exercise 43.3

Translate into English:

1. adveniam. ....

2. trademus. ....

3. ludent. ....

4. reges. ....

5. constituet. ....

6. discedemus. ....

7. punient. ....

8. ero. ....

9. iaciam. ....

10. pones. ....

Exercise 43.4

Translate into Latin:

1. fugiet. ....

2. eritis. ....

3. scribemus. ....

4. accipient. ....

5. dormiet. ....

Warning! The verbs in the following exercises are not all in the future tense.

Exercise 43.5

Translate into English:

1. currit.
2. curret.
3. regimus.
4. regemus.
5. festinabit.
6. festinamus.
7. est.
8. erit.
9. clamabit.
10. bibet.

Exercise 43.6

Translate into Latin:

1. We sleep.
2. We enter.
3. You (pl) will laugh.
4. You (sg) will read.
5. I shall have.
6. They will arrive.
7. She will flee.
8. She flees.
9. They capture.
10. You (pl) will have.

Exercise 43.7

Translate into English:

1. heri servus laborabat.
2. hodie servus laborat.
3. cras servus fugiet.
4. heri oppidum oppugnabamus.
5. hodie oppidum oppugnamus.
6. cras oppidum capiemus.
7. heri pueri currebant.
8. hodie pueri currunt.
9. cras pueri current.
10. pueri magistros numquam audient.

Exercise 43.8

Translate into Latin (use the Handy Vocabulary below to help):

1. Many young men will arrive tomorrow.
2. Help will come soon.
3. My father will be making a long journey.
4. The angry prisoners will attack the walls.
5. The boys will hurry to the city.

Handy Vocabulary for Exercise 43.8

angry	iratus, -a, -um	long	longus, -a, -um
arrive	advenio, -ire, -veni (4)	make	facio, -ere, feci (3½)
attack	oppugno, -are, -avi (1)	many	multi, -ae, -a
boy	puer, pueri m.	my	meus, -a, -um
city	urbs, urbis f.	slave	servus, -i m.
come	venio, -ire, veni (4)	soon	mox
father	pater, patris m.	to(wards)	ad + accusative
help	auxilium, -i n.	tomorrow	cras
hurry	festino, -are, -avi (1)	wall	murus, -i m.
journey	iter, itineris n.	young man	iuvenis, -is m.

Chapter 44: The Story of Troy (Part 5)
ubi and *quamquam* clauses

Exercise 44.1

Venus wins and promises Paris Helen, wife of Menelaus of Sparta.

1 postero die tres deae ad Paridem iterum venerunt. ante Paridem steterunt. Paridi haec verba dixerunt:

'Pari, deam pulcherrimam nunc legere debes.'

Paris, quamquam iram dearum timebat, clamavit:

5 'ego Venerem lego. Venus super omnes alias dea pulcherrima est.'

Venus, ubi verba Paridis audivit, risit. laeta erat. Iuno tamen et Minerva, propter verba Paridis, non riserunt. non laetae erant. iratae discesserunt.

Paris Venerem spectavit. 'ego,' inquit, 'te legi. mulierem
10 pulcherrimam uxorem cupio. ubi est?'

Venus Paridi respondit:

'mulier pulcherrima Helena est. in Graecia in oppido Sparta cum marito Menelao habitat. naviga ad Graeciam, cape Helenam, eam ad urbem Troiam reduc! sic mulier pulcherrima tua uxor erit.'

postero die = on the next day
Paris, Paridis m. = Paris
ante + acc. = before
haec = these
pulcherrimus, -a, -um = most beautiful
debeo, -ere, debui + infin. (2) = I must, have to
quamquam = although
Venus, Veneris f. = Venus
super omnes alias = above all others
Iuno = Juno
propter + acc. = because of
mulier, mulieris f. = woman
uxorem = as my wife

eam = her
reduco, -ere, -duxi (3) = I lead/take back

(a copy of this passage in workbook format can be found on page 70.)

Exercise 44.2

1. From the passage above, give, in Latin, an example of:

   a. a verb in the perfect tense; ....

   b. a verb in the imperfect tense; ....

   c. a preposition. ....

2. **risit** (line 6). For this verb, give:

   a. its person; ....

   b. its number; ....

   c. the first person singular of its present tense. ....

3. **verba** (line 6). Give the gender of this noun. ....

4. **Paridi** (line 11). Give the case of this noun. ....

5. **Graeciam** (line 13).

   a. In which case is this noun? ....

   b. Why is this case used? ....

Vocabulary Box 31a	
ante + acc.	before
mulier, mulieris f.	woman
propter + acc	because of
quamquam	although
super + acc.	above

Vocabulary Box 31b	
above	super + acc.
although	quamquam
because of	propter + acc.
before	ante + acc.
woman	mulier, mulieris f.

Practising *ubi* (when) ... and *quamquam* (although ...) clauses

Latin likes to start a sentence with the subject of the verb, but <u>sometimes</u> it will result in better English if you delay the subject and move the *when* or *although* to the <u>beginning</u> of your sentence.

Exercise 44.3

Translate into English:

1. domina, quamquam magnam pecuniam habebat, non laeta erat.

....

2. iuvenes, quamquam iter longum non erat, fessi erant.

....

3. mulier, quamquam pulchra erat, maritum non habebat.

....

4. Graeci, quamquam bene pugnaverunt, Romanos non superaverunt.

....

5. quamquam undae magnae erant, nautae non timebant.

....

Exercise 44.4

Translate into English:

1. pueri, ubi diu laboraverunt, fessi erant.

....

2. ubi parentes meos vidi, laetus eram.

....

3. nautae, ubi ad insulam advenerunt, templa spectare cupiebant.

....

4. ubi ad urbem advenimus, ibi diu mansimus.

....

5. Romani, ubi Graecos superaverunt, urbem ceperunt.

....

Chapter 45: The Story of Troy (Part 6)
Verb revision

Exercise 45.1

Paris leaves Troy, goes to the Greek city of Sparta and kidnaps Menelaus' wife Helen.

1 Helena mulier pulchra et clara erat. in urbe Sparta cum marito, Menelao nomine, habitabat. Paris vir clarus erat. in urbe Troia habitabat. Troia erat urbs in Asia <u>sita</u>.

> sita = situated

5 Paris ex urbe Troia ad urbem Spartam navigavit. ubi advenit, e <u>nave</u> <u>descendit</u> et ad <u>regiam</u> festinavit. ibi puella Helena Paridem salutavit. Paris, ubi Helenam vidit, <u>eam</u> statim amavit.

> navis, navis f. = ship
> descendit = disembarked, got off
> regia, -ae f. = palace
> eam = her

Paris Helenae 'te amo', inquit, 'Helena. veni! ex Graecia navigabimus et ego te ad urbem Troiam ducam! festina!'

10 Paris Helenam ad <u>navem</u> duxit. deinde celeriter <u>fugerunt</u>. Paris et Helena ad urbem Troiam navigaverunt. Paris laetus erat. Menelaus <u>autem</u>, maritus Helenae, non laetus sed <u>iratissimus</u> erat.

> fugio, -ere, fugi (3½) = I flee
> autem = however
> iratissimus = very angry

(a copy of this passage in workbook format can be found on page 71.)

Exercise 45.2

1. From the passage above, give, in Latin, an example of:

   a. a conjunction; ....

   b. an adverb. ....

2. **urbe** (line 1).

   a. In which case is this noun? ....

   b. Why is this case used? ....

3. **nomine** (line 2). Explain the connection between this word and the English word *nominate*.

   ....

   ....

   ....

4. **ducam** (line 8). For this verb, give:

   a. its person; ....

   b. its number; ....

   c. its tense; ....

   d. the first person singular of its present tense. ....

Vocabulary Box 33a		Vocabulary Box 33b	
autem	however	I flee	fugio, -ere, fugi (3½)
fugio, -ere, fugi (3½)	I flee	however	autem
navis, -is f.	ship	ship	navis, -is f.

Verb Revision

Quick reminder of the four tenses covered so far:

		1 *love*	2 *warn*	3 *rule*	3½ *take*	4 *hear*	irreg *be*
Present	*am/is/are*	amo	moneo	rego	capio	audio	sum
Imperfect	*was/were ~ing*	amabam	monebam	regebam	capiebam	audiebam	eram
Perfect	*did*	amavi	monui	rexi	cepi	audivi	fui
Future	*will*	amabo	monebo	regam	capiam	audiam	ero

Exercise 45.3

Translate into English:

1. fugiunt.
2. superabam.
3. oppugnabis.
4. cucurrerunt
5. constituerunt.
6. discedemus.
7. advenisti.
8. aderat.
9. iecit.
10. misimus.

Exercise 45.4

Translate into English:

1. erras.
2. superavit.
3. oppugnaverunt.
4. currebas.
5. dormiemus.
6. fuerunt.
7. constituam.
8. discedebat.
9. dabit.
10. dedit.

Exercise 45.5

Translate into Latin:

1. We shall arrive.
2. They ran.
3. He ordered.
4. They decided.
5. They were watching.
6. They fled.
7. They will sail.
8. He announced.
9. She called.
10. They were.

Exercise 45.6

Translate into Latin:

1. We shall overcome.
2. He was walking.
3. We are sailing.
4. He is arriving.
5. I shall run.
6. They fought.
7. You (pl) will send.
8. We shall flee.
9. You (sg) are standing.
10. We were laughing.

Exercise 45.7

Translate into English:

1. iussit. ....

2. ponam. ....

3. fugiemus. ....

4. cupiebamus. ....

5. timebat. ....

6. nuntiavit. ....

7. rexit. ....

8. advenio. ....

9. duxit. ....

10. iubeo ....

Exercise 45.8

Translate into English:

1. adveniam. ....

2. movemus. ....

3. mittunt. ....

4. tradidi. ....

5. posuerunt. ....

6. oppugnabatis. ....

7. dicebat. ....

8. iusserunt. ....

9. erraverunt. ....

10. damus. ....

Exercise 45.9

Translate into Latin:

1. They were building. ....

2. We were playing. ....

3. We shall see. ....

4. You (sg) will stay. ....

5. I kill. ....

6. They were approaching. ....

7. We shall drink. ....

8. He was holding. ....

9. We were throwing. ....

10. He asked. ....

Exercise 45.10

Translate into Latin:

1. I shall announce. ....

2. They answered. ....

3. I shall order. ....

4. He wrote. ....

5. He captured. ....

6. I am reading. ....

7. We were. ....

8. You (sg) built. ....

9. He punished. ....

10. We were sending. ....

Chapter 46: The Story of Troy (Part 7)

is, ea, id

Exercise 46.1

Menelaus appeals for help from other cities in Greece,
and the combined Greek forces sail to Troy, where the fighting begins.

1 Menelaus iratus erat quod Paris uxorem, Helenam nomine, ad urbem Troiam <u>duxerat</u>. Menelaus Paridem punire et Troiam delere cupiebat. <u>copias</u> igitur parare et bellum contra <u>Troianos</u> <u>gerere</u>
5 constituit.

itaque nuntios ad <u>omnes</u> urbes Graeciae misit. auxilium Graecorum rogavit. Graeci, ubi verba nuntiorum audiverunt, <u>milites</u> et naves <u>collegerunt</u> et <u>eas</u> <u>copias</u> ad Menelaum <u>sine</u> <u>mora</u> miserunt.

10 Menelaus, ubi copias Graecorum vidit, laetus erat. Graeci <u>milites</u> navesque paraverunt et trans mare ad urbem Troiam celeriter navigaverunt. sed ubi naves ad <u>litus</u> appropinquaverunt, <u>nemo</u> ex Graecis in terram <u>desilire</u> <u>primus</u> cupiebat.

15 tandem Protesilaus, <u>miles</u> Graecus, <u>primus</u> in terram <u>descendit</u>. ubi <u>is</u> <u>descendit</u>, ceteri Graeci <u>descenderunt</u>. contra Troianos <u>ruerunt</u> et multos <u>eorum</u> <u>occiderunt</u>. Protesilaus <u>autem</u>, postquam multa vulnera <u>accepit</u>, <u>primus</u> Graecus <u>occisus est</u>.

duxerat = had taken
copiae, -arum f.pl. = troops, forces
Troianus, -a, -um = Trojan
gero, -ere, gessi (3) = wage, carry on

omnes = all
miles, militis m. = soldier
colligo, -ere, collegi (3) = I collect
eas = those
sine + abl. = without
mora, -ae f. = delay
litus, -oris n. = shore
nemo = no-one
desilire = to jump down
primus = first
descendo, -ere, -di (3) = I climb down, disembark
ruo, -ere, rui (3) = charge

is = he
eorum = of them
occido, -ere, occidi (3) = I kill
autem = however
accipio, -ere, accepi (3½) = I receive
occisus est = (he) was killed

(a copy of this passage in workbook format can be found on page 70.)

Exercise 46.2

1. From the passage above, give, in Latin, an example of:

   a. a noun in the ablative case; ....

   b. an infinitive; ....

   c. a verb in the imperfect tense; ....

   d. a preposition. ....

2. **miserunt** (line 9). For this verb, give:

   a. its person;

   b. its number; ....

   c. its tense; ....

   d. the first person singular of its present tense. ....

3. **vulnera** (line 19).

   a. In which case is this noun? ....

   b. Why is this case used? ....

26

Vocabulary Box 34a	
accipio, -ere, accepi (3½)	I receive
arma, armorum n.pl.	weapons
bellum gero, -ere, gessi (3)	I wage war
colligo, -ere, collegi (3)	I collect
copiae, -arum f.pl.	forces
miles, militis m.	soldier
mora, -ae f.	delay
occido, -ere, occidi (3)	I kill
ruo, -ere, rui (3)	I charge
sine + abl.	without

Vocabulary Box 34b	
I charge	ruo, -ere, rui (3)
I collect	colligo, -ere, collegi (3)
delay	mora, -ae f.
forces	copiae, -arum f.pl.
I kill	occido, -ere, occidi (3)
I receive	accipio, -ere, accepi (3½)
soldier	miles, militis m.
I wage war	bellum gero, -ere, gessi (3)
weapons	arma, armorum n.pl.
without	sine + abl.

Third person pronoun: *is, ea, id* (= *he, she, it; that, those*)

singular	masculine		feminine		neuter	
nominative	is	*he*	ea	*she*	id	*it*
accusative	eum	*him*	eam	*her*	id	*it*
genitive	eius	*his (of him)*	eius	*her (of her)*	eius	*of it*
dative	ei	*to/for him*	ei	*to/for her*	ei	*to/for it*
ablative	eo	*by him*	ea	*by her*	eo	*by it*
plural						
nominative	ei	*they*	eae	*they*	ea	*they*
accusative	eos	*them*	eas	*them*	ea	*them*
genitive	eorum	*their (of them)*	earum	*their (of them)*	eorum	*their (of them)*
dative	eis	*to/for them*	eis	*to/for them*	eis	*to/for them*
ablative	eis	*by them*	eis	*by them*	eis	*by them*

Generally speaking, if *is, ea, id* is used in agreement with a noun, it means *that* or *those*. If not, it means *he, she, it* as in the table above.

Examples

eam puellam amo.	*I like that girl.*
eam amo.	*I like her.*
eos servos non amo.	*I do not like those slaves.*
eos non amo.	*I do not like them.*

English warning!
Beware: some masculine/feminine singular nouns in Latin are referred to as *it* in English.

Examples

gladium habeo. eum amo. *I have a sword. I like it. (not I like him.)*
villam habeo. eam amo. *I have a villa. I like it. (not I like her.)*

Exercise 46.3

Translate into English:

1. Menelaus miles Graecus erat. is vir bonus erat.
2. Menelaus uxorem habebat. nomen eius Helena erat.
3. Helena uxor Menelai erat. ea femina pulchra erat.
4. Paris eam magnopere amabat.
5. Romulus fratrem habebat. eum occidit.
6. insula magna est. multi incolae in ea habitant.
7. magister multos libros habet. eos libros saepe legit.
8. dominus servum bonum habet. pecuniam ei servo saepe dat.
9. servi eum dominum non amant.
10. Graeci multa arma habebant. arma eorum nova erant.

Exercise 46.4

Translate into English:

1. poeta librum scribit. multa verba in eo sunt.
2. rex servos suos non amat. pecuniam eis non saepe dat.
3. ei muri alti et validi erant.
4. magister eum puerum non amabat. eum igitur saepe puniebat.
5. Protesilaus fortiter pugnavit. Troiani tamen eum mox occiderunt.
6. Graeci eum militem magnopere laudaverunt.
7. is miles multa vulnera accepit. vulnera eius mala erant.
8. navis magna erat. erant in ea multi nautae.
9. milites Romani boni erant. Graeci eos non superaverunt.
10. agricolae multos agros habebant. agri eorum magni erant.

Handy Help

singular	masculine		feminine		neuter	
nominative	is	*he*	ea	*she*	id	*it*
accusative	eum	*him*	eam	*her*	id	*it*
genitive	eius	*his (of him)*	eius	*her (of her)*	eius	*of it*
dative	ei	*to/for him*	ei	*to/for her*	ei	*to/for it*
ablative	eo	*by him*	ea	*by her*	eo	*by it*
plural						
nominative	ei	*they*	eae	*they*	ea	*they*
accusative	eos	*them*	eas	*them*	ea	*them*
genitive	eorum	*their (of them)*	earum	*their (of them)*	eorum	*their (of them)*
dative	eis	*to/for them*	eis	*to/for them*	eis	*to/for them*
ablative	eis	*by them*	eis	*by them*	eis	*by them*

Exercise 46.5

Translate into English:

1. villam eius non amo.

   ....

2. ea femina pulchra erat. multi viri eam amabant.

   ....

3. urbs magna erat. Romani eam urbem capere constituerunt.

   ....

4. id vinum bonum est. id saepe bibo.

   ....

5. Graeci multa arma collegerunt. ea in navibus posuerunt.

   ....

6. Menelaus et Helena Graeci erant. is clarus, ea pulchra erat.

   ....

7. puer, quod eam puellam amabat, multa dona ei dabat.

   ....

8. quod servi boni erant, dominus magnam pecuniam eis dedit.

   ....

9. magistri multa verba saepe dicunt. pueri tamen ea non saepe audiunt.

   ....

10. auxilio eorum urbem cepimus.

    ....

Handy Help

singular	masculine		feminine		neuter	
nominative	is	*he*	ea	*she*	id	*it*
accusative	eum	*him*	eam	*her*	id	*it*
genitive	eius	*his (of him)*	eius	*her (of her)*	eius	*of it*
dative	ei	*to/for him*	ei	*to/for her*	ei	*to/for it*
ablative	eo	*by him*	ea	*by her*	eo	*by it*
plural						
nominative	ei	*they*	eae	*they*	ea	*they*
accusative	eos	*them*	eas	*them*	ea	*them*
genitive	eorum	*their (of them)*	earum	*their (of them)*	eorum	*their (of them)*
dative	eis	*to/for them*	eis	*to/for them*	eis	*to/for them*
ablative	eis	*by them*	eis	*by them*	eis	*by them*

Exercise 46.6

Translate into Latin:

1. I have a garden. I love it.

   ....

2. He has daughters. He loves them.

   ....

3. I am reading a book. I like it.

   ....

4. We are looking at those temples.

   ....

5. They do not like that teacher.

   ....

Exercise 46.7

Translate into Latin:

1. She prepares food for them.

   ....

2. I am giving gold to that man.

   ....

3. The master punished them.

   ....

4. I ran towards her.

   ....

5. We saw that man near the villa.

   ....

Handy Help

singular	masculine		feminine		neuter	
nominative	is	*he*	ea	*she*	id	*it*
accusative	eum	*him*	eam	*her*	id	*it*
genitive	eius	*his (of him)*	eius	*her (of her)*	eius	*of it*
dative	ei	*to/for him*	ei	*to/for her*	ei	*to/for it*
ablative	eo	*by him*	ea	*by her*	eo	*by it*
plural						
nominative	ei	*they*	eae	*they*	ea	*they*
accusative	eos	*them*	eas	*them*	ea	*them*
genitive	eorum	*their (of them)*	earum	*their (of them)*	eorum	*their (of them)*
dative	eis	*to/for them*	eis	*to/for them*	eis	*to/for them*
ablative	eis	*by them*	eis	*by them*	eis	*by them*

Chapter 47: The Story of Troy (Part 8)
The pluperfect tense

Exercise 47.1

The Greeks realise that capturing Troy will not be a five-minute job.
The Greek warrior Achilles wants to take revenge on the Trojan Hector.

1 Protesilaus <u>mortuus</u> erat. Graeci contra muros Troiae <u>ruerant</u>. <u>sub</u> muris fortiter <u>pugnaverant</u>, sed <u>frustra</u>. non multos Troianos <u>vulneraverant</u>. urbem non <u>ceperant</u>. Agamemnon, frater Menelai, <u>dux</u> Graecorum erat. non laetus erat. <u>haec</u> verba militibus dixit:

5 'comites <u>cari</u>, <u>hostes</u> hodie non superavimus. muri Troiae alti et validi sunt. <u>cives</u> Troiani <u>fortes</u> sunt. muros urbis bene <u>defendunt</u>. <u>castra</u> ponite! bene dormite! cras contra hostes iterum pugnabimus. sine <u>dubio</u> bellum longum erit.'

diu copiae Graecorum muros Troiae oppugnaverunt. eos tamen
10 delere non <u>poterant</u>. rex Troiae Priamus erat. multos <u>liberos</u> claros habebat. <u>inter</u> eos erat Hector. is semper magna <u>virtute</u> <u>pro</u> Troianis pugnabat. numquam <u>mortem</u> timebat.

<u>inter</u> Graecos <u>quoque</u> erant multi milites <u>fortes</u>. Achilles autem <u>fortissimus</u> erat. amicum <u>carum</u>, Patroclum nomine, habebat.
15 quod Hector Patroclum in proelio <u>occiderat</u>, Achilles <u>iratissimus</u> erat. Hectorem necare magnopere cupiebat.

ruerant = had charged
mortuus, -a, -um = dead
sub + abl. = under
pugnaverant = had fought
frustra = in vain
vulneraverant = had wounded
ceperant = had captured
dux, ducis m. = leader
haec = these
comes, comitis m. = comrade
carus, -a, -um = dear
hostes, -ium m.pl. = enemy
civis, civis m. = citizen
fortes = brave
defendo, -ere, defendi (3) = I defend
castra, -orum n.pl. = camp
dubium, -i n. = doubt
poterant = they were able
liberi, -orum m.pl. = children
inter + acc. = between, among
quoque = also
virtus, virtutis m. = bravery
pro + abl. = for
mors, mortis f. = death
fortissimus = the bravest
occiderat = had killed
iratissimus = very angry

(a copy of this passage in workbook format can be found on page 73.)

Exercise 47.2

1. From the passage above, give, in Latin, an example of:

   a. an imperative; ....

   b. an adverb; ....

   c. a verb in the future tense; ....

   d. a noun in the genitive case. ....

2. **dixit** (line 4). For this verb, give:

   a. its person; ....

   b. its number; ....

   c. its tense; ....

   d. the first person singular of its present tense. ....

3. **proelio** (line 15).

   a. In which case is this noun? ....

   b. Why is this case used? ....

Vocabulary Box 35a	
carus, -a, -um	dear
civis, civis m.	citizen
comes, comitis m.	comrade
defendo, -ere, defendi (3)	I defend
dux, ducis m.	leader, general
frustra	in vain
hostes, hostium m.pl	enemy
inter + acc.	between, among
is, ea, id	he, she, it; that
liberi, -orum m.pl. *(*see note below)*	children
mors, mortis f.	death
mortuus, -a, -um	dead
pro + abl.	for
quoque	also
sub + abl.	under
virtus, virtutis f.	bravery

Vocabulary Box 35b	
also	quoque
between, among	inter + acc.
bravery	virtus, virtutis f.
children	liberi, -orum m.pl. *(*see note below)*
citizen	civis, civis, m.
comrade	comes, comitis m.
dead	mortuus, -a, -um
dear	carus, -a, -um
death	mors, mortis f.
enemy	hostes, hostium m.pl.
he, she, it; that	is, ea, id
I defend	defendo, -ere, defendi (3)
for	pro + abl.
in vain	frustra
leader, general	dux, ducis m.
under	sub + abl.

* **Note:** This word keeps its *e*. Beware of confusing it with the plural of books (*libri*), which doesn't! Compare the tables below.

		book	children
singular	nominative	liber	
	vocative	liber	
	accusative	librum	
	genitive	libri	
	dative	libro	
	ablative	libro	
plural	nominative	libri	liberi
	vocative	libri	liberi
	accusative	libros	liberos
	genitive	librorum	liberorum
	dative	libris	liberis
	ablative	libris	liberis

The Pluperfect Tense

This is the *had* tense. It is formed by taking the perfect stem (that is, removing the *-i* from the **third** principal part of the verb) and adding these personal endings:

-eram	I had done something
-eram	You (sg) had done something
-erat	He/She/It had done something
-eramus	We had done something
-eratis	You (pl) had done something
-erant	They had done something

Using our model verbs:

1	amo, amare, **amavi**
2	moneo, monere, **monui**
3	rego, regere, **rexi**
4	audio, audire, **audivi**
to be	sum, esse, **fui**

this gives us:

	1 *… loved*	**2** *… warned*
I had …	amav**eram**	monu**eram**
You (sg) had …	amav**eras**	monu**eras**
He/She/It had …	amav**erat**	monu**erat**
We had …	amav**eramus**	monu**eramus**
You (pl) had …	amav**eratis**	monu**eratis**
They had …	amav**erant**	monu**erant**

	3 *… ruled*	**3½** *… taken*
I had …	rex**eram**	cep**eram**
You (sg) had …	rex**eras**	cep**eras**
He/She/It had …	rex**erat**	cep**erat**
We had …	rex**eramus**	cep**eramus**
You (pl) had …	rex**eratis**	cep**eratis**
They had …	rex**erant**	cep**erant**

	4 *… heard*	**sum** *… been*
I had …	audiv**eram**	fu**eram**
You (sg) had …	audiv**eras**	fu**eras**
He/She/It had …	audiv**erat**	fu**erat**
We had …	audiv**eramus**	fu**eramus**
You (pl) had …	audiv**eratis**	fu**eratis**
They had …	audiv**erant**	fu**erant**

Exercise 47.3

Translate into English:

1. amaveramus.
2. ceperant.
3. audiveras.
4. rexerat.
5. dederam.
6. duxerat.
7. moveramus.
8. terruerat.
9. responderant.
10. miseram.

Exercise 47.4

Translate into English:

1. posuerat.
2. cucurrerant.
3. discesseras.
4. legeram.
5. dormiveramus.
6. ambulaveramus.
7. feceratis.
8. riseramus.
9. fugerat.
10. deleveras.

Exercise 47.5

Translate into Latin:

1. He had loved.
2. They had carried.
3. We had remained.
4. I had seen.
5. You (sg) had sent.
6. They had put.
7. We had made.
8. You (pl) had taken.
9. They had heard.
10. I had come.

Exercise 47.6

Translate into Latin:

1. She had slept.
2. He had punished.
3. You (sg) had played.
4. He had given.
5. They had laughed.
6. We had fought.
7. They had departed.
8. I had read.
9. We had destroyed.
10. He had walked.

Handy Help

I carry	porto, portare, portavi (1)		I play	ludo, ludere, lusi (3)
I come	venio, venire, veni (4)		I punish	punio, punire, punivi (4)
I depart	discedo, discedere, discessi (3)		I put	pono, ponere, posui (3)
I destroy	deleo, delere, delevi (2)		I read	lego, legere, legi (3)
I fight	pugno, pugnare, pugnavi (1)		I remain	maneo, manere, mansi (2)
I give	do, dare, dedi (1)		I see	video, videre, vidi (2)
I hear	audio, audire, audivi (4)		I send	mitto, mittere, misi (3)
I fight	pugno, pugnare, pugnavi (1)		I sleep	dormio, dormire, dormivi (4)
I laugh	rideo, ridere, risi (2)		I take	capio, capere, cepi (3 ½)
I love	amo, amare, amavi (1)		I walk	ambulo, ambulare, ambulavi (1)
I make	facio, facere, feci (3½)			

Exercise 47.7

Translate into English:

1. manseramus. ....

2. viderant. ....

3. intraverant. ....

4. ceperat. ....

5. monueras. ....

6. biberat. ....

7. dixerat. ....

8. luseramus. ....

9. occideratis. ....

10. pugnaverat. ....

Exercise 47.8

Translate into Latin:

1. They had made. ....

2. He had seen. ....

3. You (sg) had destroyed. ....

4. We had put. ....

5. I had laughed. ....

6. You (pl) had punished. ....

7. He had made. ....

8. We had come. ....

9. She had sent. ....

10. They had taken. ....

Exercise 47.9

Translate into English:

1. pueri mali fuerant.

   ....

2. ancillae cenam non bene paraverant.

   ....

3. magister iratus erat quod riseramus.

   ....

4. puella puerum vulneraverat.

   ....

5. verba non audiveramus.

   ....

Exercise 47.10

Translate into Latin:

1. We had overcome the enemy.

   ....

2. They had captured the city.

   ....

3. He had killed the freedman.

   ....

4. I had seen the girl.

   ....

5. We had defended the town.

   ....

Handy Help

	Nouns		Verbs
enemy	hostes, hostium m.pl.	I capture	capio, -ere, cepi (3½)
city	urbs, urbis f.	I defend	defendo, -ere, defendi (3)
freedman	libertus, -i m.	I kill	occido, -ere, occidi (3)
girl	puella, puellae f.	I overcome	supero, -are, superavi (1)
town	oppidum, -i n.	I see	video, -ere, vidi (2)

Exercise 47.11

Translate into English:

1. proelium longum fuerat.

   ....

2. tandem is ducem occiderat.

   ....

3. Graeci multa oppida ceperant.

   ....

4. puer donum ad patrem miserat.

   ....

5. milites non bene pugnaverant.

   ....

6. cives oppidum fortiter defenderant.

   ....

7. hostes laeti erant quod Romani discesserant.

   ....

8. puer celeriter cucurrit quod magistrum iratum viderat.

   ....

9. maritus malus uxorem vulneraverat.

   ....

10. miles multa vulnera acceperat.

   ....

Exercise 47.12

Translate into Latin:

1. The teacher had said many words.

   ....

2. The Greeks had collected many weapons.

   ....

3. The enemy had charged against the city.

   ....

4. The soldier had killed the slave with a spear.

   ....

5. The slavegirls had looked at the ships for a long time.

   ....

Chapter 48: The Story of Troy (Part 9)
Third declension adjectives in -*is* (*fortis*)

Exercise 48.1

Achilles, angry because of Patroclus' death, tells Hector he will kill him.
Hector is not impressed.

1   Achilles iratus erat quod Hector Patroclum occiderat. Hectorem igitur occidere cupiebat.

olim Troiani contra Graecos prope urbem Troiam pugnabant. omnes fortiter pugnabant. tum subito Achilles Hectorem in
5   proelio forte conspexit. ubi eum vidit, ei clamavit:

'audi me, Hector! ego sum Achilles, fortissimus Graecorum. tu vir crudelis es. quod tu Patroclum, amicum meum, occidisti, ego te occidam!'

Hector, ubi verba Achillis audivit, ei respondit:

10   'audi verba mea, Achilles! laetus sum quod ego Patroclum, amicum tuum, occidi. ego te non timeo. tu me non terres! tu fortis non es. tu audax non es. tu nobilis non es! veni! pugna! victoria mihi non difficilis sed facilis erit. ego te mox vincam!'

omnes = everyone
tum = then
forte = by chance
conspicio, -ere, conspexi, conspectum (3 ½) = I catch sight of
fortissimus = the bravest
crudelis = cruel

fortis = brave
audax = bold, daring
nobilis = noble
victoria, -ae f. = victory
mihi = for me
difficilis = difficult
facilis = easy
vinco, -ere, vici (3) = I conquer

(a copy of this passage in workbook format can be found on page 74.)

Exercise 48.2

1. From the passage above, give, in Latin, an example of:

    a. a verb in the pluperfect tense;

    ....

    b. an adverb;

    ....

    c. an imperative;

    ....

    d. a neuter noun.

    ....

2. **ei** (line 5). Give the nominative masculine singular of this pronoun

    ....

3. **occidam** (line 8). For this verb, give:

    a. its person;

    ....

    b. its number;

    ....

    c. its tense.

    ....

4. **vincam** (line 13). Explain the connection between this word and the English word *invincible*.

....

....

Third declension adjectives in -is

e.g. fortis, *brave*

		masculine	feminine	neuter
singular	nominative	fort**is**	fort**is**	fort**e**
	vocative	fort**is**	fort**is**	fort**e**
	accusative	fort**em**	fort**em**	fort**e**
	genitive	fort**is**	fort**is**	fort**is**
	dative	fort**i**	fort**i**	fort**i**
	ablative	fort**i**	fort**i**	fort**i**
plural	nominative	fort**es**	fort**es**	fort**ia**
	vocative	fort**es**	fort**es**	fort**ia**
	accusative	fort**es**	fort**es**	fort**ia**
	genitive	fort**ium**	fort**ium**	fort**ium**
	dative	fort**ibus**	fort**ibus**	fort**ibus**
	ablative	fort**ibus**	fort**ibus**	fort**ibus**

(You will see similarities here with the tables of rex, regis m. *king* and opus, operis n. *task*. But beware of the ablative singular in **-i**, not **-e**, which you might expect!)

Vocabulary Box 36a		**Vocabulary Box 36b**	
crudelis, -is, -e	cruel	all, every	omnis, -is, -e
difficilis, -is, -e	difficult	brave	fortis, -is, -e
facilis, -is, -e	easy	cruel	crudelis, -is, -e
fortis, -is, -e	brave	difficult	difficilis, -is, -e
nobilis, -is, -e	noble	easy	facilis, -is, -e
omnis, -is, -e *(see note 1 below)*	all, every	noble	nobilis, -is, -e
tristis, -is, -e	sad	sad	tristis, -is, -e
conspicio, -ere, conspexi (3½)	I catch sight of	I catch sight of	conspicio, -ere, conspexi (3½)
forte *(see note 2 below)*	by chance	I conquer	vinco, -ere, vici (3)
tum	then	by chance	forte
vinco, -ere, vici (3)	conquer	then	tum

Notes on Vocabulary Box 36

1. **omnis**, when linked with a plural noun, which is common, is translated as *all:*

      omnes pueri timebant.   *All the boys were afraid.*

When linked with a singular noun (which is less common), it is translated as *every:*

      omnis puer timebat.   *Every boy was afraid.*

When *omnes* (m.pl.) is not linked to any noun it simply means *everyone:*

      omnes timebant.   *Everyone was afraid.*

When *omnia* (n.pl.) is not linked to any noun it simply means *everything:*

      omnia facio.   *I do everything.*

2. **forte** is the ablative singular of the third declension noun noun *fors* (= chance, luck). Beware of confusing this with the neuter singular of the adjective *fortis* (= brave).

Exercise 48.3

Translate into English:

1. rex nobilis
2. reges nobiles
3. liber difficilis
4. itinera difficilia
5. milites fortes
6. omnia scuta
7. omnes puellae
8. viri tristes
9. miles fortis
10. vulnera crudelia

Exercise 48.4

Translate into Latin:

1. an easy journey
2. difficult books
3. a difficult war
4. a sad girl
5. cruel masters
6. all the soldiers
7. easy journeys
8. a brave husband
9. sad women
10. all wines

Exercise 48.5

Translate into English:

1. dominum crudelem habeo.
2. iter facile facio.
3. omnia vina amo.
4. omnes libros lego.
5. omnes puellas specto.
6. omnia non porto.
7. librum difficilem lego.
8. ducem fortem saluto.
9. servum tristem video.
10. omnes pueros laudo.

Exercise 48.6

Translate into Latin:

1. I am setting free the brave slave.
2. I like all girls.
3. I do not like everyone.
4. I like difficult books.
5. I am killing the cruel master.
6. I am afraid of the cruel soldiers.
7. I praise brave soldiers.
8. I am doing a difficult journey.
9. I am carrying all the weapons.
10. I hear cruel words.

Exercise 48.7

Translate into English:

1. is rex nobilis est.
2. cur tristis es, puer?
3. tristis sum quod magister crudelis est.
4. omnes pueri laborant.
5. non omnes servi difficiles sunt.

Exercise 48.8

Translate into Latin:

1. by an easy road
2. to the cruel husband
3. by cruel wounds
4. of all the girls
5. for the noble master

Exercise 48.9

Translate into English:

1. omnes puellae ludunt.

   ....

2. librum facilem legimus.

   ....

3. non omnes magistri crudeles sunt.

   ....

4. servi tristes dominum crudelem timent.

   ....

5. eum librum difficilem non amo.

   ....

6. frater meus omnia parat.

   ....

7. itinera difficilia saepe facimus.

   ....

8. magister crudelis omnes pueros punit.

   ....

9. dominus nobilis servos laudat.

   ....

10. servi tristes sunt quod dominus saepe crudelis est.

   ....

Exercise 48.10

Translate into Latin:

1. All the boys like wine.

   ....

2. We shall overcome all the enemy.

   ....

3. The soldiers' wounds were cruel.

   ....

4. The brave citizens fought against the enemy.

   ....

5. The journey was not easy but difficult.

   ....

Chapter 49: The Story of Troy (Part 10)
Third declension adjectives like *audax* and *ingens*

Exercise 49.1

Achilles fights Hector.

1 Achilles Hectorem spectabat. Hector Achillem spectabat. Hector vir fortis et <u>audax</u> erat. Achilles tamen <u>fortior</u> et <u>audacior</u> <u>quam</u> Hector erat.

subito Hector <u>telum</u> suum iecit. <u>telum</u> ad Achillem <u>celeriter</u>
5 <u>volavit</u>. in scuto tamen Achillis <u>haesit</u>. eum non <u>vulneraverat</u>. Achilles, ubi <u>hoc</u> vidit, risit. deinde, <u>antequam</u> suum <u>telum</u> iecit, Hectori verba crudelia magna <u>voce</u> dixit: 'tu me non occidisti, Hector. <u>nemo</u> <u>fortior</u> est <u>quam</u> ego. ego sum <u>fortissimus</u> omnium Graecorum. <u>nihil</u> timeo.'

10 ubi <u>haec</u> verba dixit, sine mora <u>telum</u> ad Hectorem iecit. <u>telum</u> ad Hectorem <u>celeriter</u> <u>volavit</u> et in corpore eius <u>haesit</u>. Hector ad terram <u>cecidit</u> mortuus. Achilles <u>laetissimus</u> erat. risit.

audax = bold, daring
fortior = braver
audacior = more daring
quam = than
telum, -i n. = spear
celeriter = quickly
volo, -are, volavi (1) = I fly
haereo, -ere, haesi (2) = I stick
vulnero, -are, -avi (1) = I wound
hoc = this
antequam = before
vox, vocis f. = voice
nemo = no-one
fortissimus = the bravest
nihil = nothing
haec = these
cado, -ere, cecidi (3) = I fall
laetissimus = very happy

(a copy of this passage in workbook format can be found on page 75.)

Exercise 49.2

1. From the passage above, give, in Latin, an example of:

   a. a conjugation; ....

   b. a verb in the imperfect tense; ....

   c. a personal pronoun. ....

2. **iecit** (line 4). Explain the connection between this word and the English word *trajectory*.

   ....

   ....

   ....

3. **Achillis** (line 6). Give the case of this noun. ....

4. **risit** (line 12). For this verb, give:

   a. its person; ....

   b. its number; ....

   c. its tense; ....

   d. the first person singular of its present tense. ....

Vocabulary Box 37a	
antequam	before
celeriter	quickly
nemo	noone
nihil	nothing
quam	than
vox, vocis f.	voice
vulnero, -are, -avi (1)	I wound

Vocabulary Box 37b	
before	antequam
noone	nemo
nothing	nihil
quickly	celeriter
than	quam
voice	vox, vocis f.
I wound	vulnero, -are, -avi (1)

Third declension adjectives in -x

e.g. audax, audacis *bold, daring*

		masculine	feminine	neuter
singular	nominative	auda**x**	auda**x**	auda**x**
	vocative	auda**x**	auda**x**	auda**x**
	accusative	audac**em**	audac**em**	auda**x**
	genitive	audac**is**	audac**is**	audac**is**
	dative	audac**i**	audac**i**	audac**i**
	ablative	audac**i**	audac**i**	audac**i**
plural	nominative	audac**es**	audac**es**	audac**ia**
	vocative	audac**es**	audac**es**	audac**ia**
	accusative	audac**es**	audac**es**	audac**ia**
	genitive	audac**ium**	audac**ium**	audac**ium**
	dative	audac**ibus**	audac**ibus**	audac**ibus**
	ablative	audac**ibus**	audac**ibus**	audac**ibus**

If you compare this carefully with the table of *fortis*, which we met on page 39 – it's repeated below – you will see that the endings of these two sorts of adjectives are not miles apart.

		masculine	feminine	neuter
singular	nominative	for**tis**	for**tis**	for**te**
	vocative	for**tis**	for**tis**	for**te**
	accusative	for**tem**	for**tem**	for**te**
	genitive	for**tis**	for**tis**	for**tis**
	dative	for**ti**	for**ti**	for**ti**
	ablative	for**ti**	for**ti**	for**ti**
plural	nominative	for**tes**	for**tes**	for**tia**
	vocative	for**tes**	for**tes**	for**tia**
	accusative	for**tes**	for**tes**	for**tia**
	genitive	for**tium**	for**tium**	for**tium**
	dative	for**tibus**	for**tibus**	for**tibus**
	ablative	for**tibus**	for**tibus**	for**tibus**

The only other adjective like *audax* that you need to know at the moment is *felix, felicis* (lucky, fortunate). And the only other sort of third declension adjective you need to know at the moment is the one ending in *-ns*, like *ingens, ingentis* (huge). This is on the next page.

Third declension adjectives in -ns

e.g. ingens, ingentis *huge*

		masculine	feminine	neuter
singular	nominative	inge**ns**	inge**ns**	inge**ns**
	vocative	inge**ns**	inge**ns**	inge**ns**
	accusative	ingent**em**	ingent**em**	inge**ns**
	genitive	ingent**is**	ingent**is**	ingent**is**
	dative	ingent**i**	ingent**i**	ingent**i**
	ablative	ingent**i**	ingent**i**	ingent**i**
plural	nominative	ingent**es**	ingent**es**	ingent**ia**
	vocative	ingent**es**	ingent**es**	ingent**ia**
	accusative	ingent**es**	ingent**es**	ingent**ia**
	genitive	ingent**ium**	ingent**ium**	ingent**ium**
	dative	ingent**ibus**	ingent**ibus**	ingent**ibus**
	ablative	ingent**ibus**	ingent**ibus**	ingent**ibus**

Here is a summary of the vocabulary these two sorts of adjectives:

Vocabulary Box 38a	
audax, audacis	bold, daring
felix, felicis	lucky, fortunate
ingens, ingentis	huge
sapiens, sapientis	wise

Vocabulary Box 38b	
bold, daring	audax, audacis
lucky, fortunate	felix, felicis
huge	ingens, ingentis
wise	sapiens, sapientis

Exercise 49.3

Translate into English:

1. miles fortis
2. domina crudelis
3. templum ingens
4. pueri felices
5. magistri sapientes
6. verba sapientia
7. dux audax
8. bellum triste
9. proelia difficilia
10. servus felix

Exercise 49.4

Translate into Latin:

1. a huge task
2. difficult masters
3. cruel brothers
4. all the soldiers
5. all the words
6. a wise word
7. huge gardens
8. brave slaves
9. a bold king
10. daring girls

Handy Help

brother	frater, fratris m.	slave	servus, -i m.
garden	hortus, -i m.	soldier	miles, militis m.
girl	puella, -ae f.	task	opus, operis n.
king	rex, regis m.	word	verbum, -i n.
master	dominus, -i m.		

Exercise 49.5

Translate into English:

1. dominus servum sapientem laudat.

   ....

2. non omnes reges crudeles sunt.

   ....

3. ea puella fratrem sapientem habet.

   ....

4. omnes magistri sapientes sunt.

   ....

5. iter longum et difficile facimus.

   ....

6. omnes milites ducem felicem amant.

   ....

7. Graeci multa templa ingentia aedificabant.

   ....

8. dux sapiens milites fortes semper laudat.

   ....

9. omnes milites Romani audaces erant.

   ....

10. pueri sapientes libros difficiles saepe legunt.

   ....

Exercise 49.6

Translate into Latin:

1. I have a wise father.

   ....

2. All the slaves are working well.

   ....

3. Not all men are wise.

   ....

4. My husband is reading a difficult book.

   ....

5. We like the beautiful temple's huge walls.

   ....

Chapter 50: The Story of Troy (Part 11)
Comparison of adjectives

Exercise 50.1

Achilles mistreats Hector's body. Hector's brother, Paris, takes revenge.

1   nemo <u>crudelior</u> quam Achilles erat. is corpus Hectoris <u>currui</u> suo <u>pedibus</u> <u>vinxit</u>. deinde <u>currum</u> <u>circum</u> muros Troiae <u>egit</u>, corpus Hectoris <u>trahens</u>. propter id omnes cives Troiani <u>tristissimi</u> et <u>iratissimi</u> erant.

5   Paris frater Hectoris erat. iratus erat quod Achilles Hectorem occiderat, arma cepit, ex urbe cucurrit, in proelium ruit. Achillem statim necare cupiebat. mox eum <u>invenit</u>. tum ei clamavit:

   'Achilles, vir <u>pessimus</u> es. nemo <u>peior</u> est quam tu.
10 Hectorem, fratrem meum, occidisti. ego tamen miles <u>melior</u> sum quam tu. numquam <u>effugies</u>. nemo te <u>servare</u> <u>poterit</u>. te nunc occidam.'

   Paris <u>telum</u> in Achillem misit. <u>telum</u> in <u>calce</u> Achillis <u>haesit</u>. Achilles ad terram mortuus <u>cecidit</u>.

crudelior = more cruel
currui = dative of currus = chariot
pes, pedis m. = foot
vincio, -ire, vinxi (4) = I tie
circum + acc. = around
trahens = dragging
tristissimus, a -um = very sad
iratissimus, -a, -um = very angry

invenio, -ire, -veni (4) = I find

pessimus, -a, -um = very wicked
peior, peioris = more wicked
melior, melioris = better
effugio, -ere, effugi (3½) =
  I escape
servo, -are, -avi (1) = I save
poterit = will be able
calx, calcis f. = heel
haereo, -ere, haesi (2) = I stick
cado, -ere, cecidi (3) = I fall, drop

(a copy of this passage in workbook format can be found on page 76.)

Exercise 50.2

1. From the passage above, give, in Latin, an example of:

    a. a part of the verb *to be*;

    b. a neuter noun;

    c. a personal pronoun;

    d. a preposition.

2. **id** (line 3). Give the nominative masculine singular form of this pronoun.

3. **misit** (line 13). For this verb, give:

    a. its person;

    b. its number;

    c. its tense.

4. **calce** (line 13).

    a. In which case is this noun?

    b. Why is this case used?

Vocabulary Box 39a		Vocabulary Box 39b	
circum + acc.	around	around	circum + acc.
effugio, -ere, effugi (3½)	I escape	I escape	effugio, -ere, effugi (3½)
invenio, -ire, -veni (4)	I find	I find	invenio, -ire, -veni (4)
servo, -are, -avi (1)	I save	I save	servo, -are, -avi (1)

Comparison in English

Comparison is all about comparing things. There are three degrees of comparison. These are called *positive*, *comparative* and *superlative*.

All the adjectives you have met so far are **positive** adjectives. For example: *bonus* (good), *pulcher* (beautiful), *fortis* (brave), *ingens* (huge).

Comparative adjectives in English usually end in *-er* or start with *more*:
Examples: tall__er__, small__er__, __more__ beautiful, __more__ interesting

Superlative adjectives in English usually end in *-est* or start with *very* or *most*:
Examples: tall__est__, small__est__, __very__ beautiful, __most__ interesting

However, in English there are some irregular examples. Study these:

Positive	Comparative	Superlative
good	better (not *gooder*!)	best/very good (not *goodest*!)
bad	worse (not *badder*!)	worst/very bad (not *baddest*!)
many	more (not *manyer*!)	most/very many (not *manyest*!)

Comparison in Latin

This is how it works:

	Positive	Comparative	Superlative
-us	Formation: altus *high*	stem + **ior** altior *higher*	stem + **issimus** altissimus *very high/highest*
-er	Formation: miser *miserable* pulcher *beautiful*	stem + **ior** miserior *more miserable* pulchrior *more beautiful*	positive + **rimus** miserrimus *very/most miserable* pulcherrimus *very/most beautiful*
-is -x -ns	Formation: fortis *brave* audax *daring* ingens *huge*	stem + **ior** fortior *braver* audacior *more daring* ingentior *more huge*	stem + **issimus** fortissimus *very brave/bravest* audacissimus *very/most daring* ingentissimus *very huge*
Note!	facilis *easy* difficilis *difficult*	facilior *easier* difficilior *more difficult*	facillimus *very easy/easiest* difficillimus *very/most difficult*

Notes
You have already met the positive adjectives in this table.
The superlative adjectives all end in *-us* and have endings like *bonus*.
The comparative adjectives all end in *-ior*. Their endings are like those of *fortior*, which appears on the next page.

Irregular Comparisons

Like English, Latin has a few irregulars. These five are very common and should be learned by heart (you may well be able to think of some connections with English to help you with this):

Positive	Comparative	Superlative
bonus *good*	melior *better*	optimus *very good, best*
malus *bad*	peior *worse*	pessimus *very bad, worst*
magnus *big*	maior *bigger*	maximus *very big, biggest*
parvus *small*	minor *smaller*	minimus *very small, smallest*
multus *much, many*	plus *more* *(see note below)*	plurimus *very many, most*

Third declension comparative adjectives in *-or*

e.g. fortior, fortioris *braver*

		masculine	feminine	neuter
singular	nominative	fort**ior**	fort**ior**	fort**ius** (!)
	vocative	fort**ior**	fort**ior**	fort**ius** (!)
	accusative	fortior**em**	fortior**em**	fort**ius** (!)
	genitive	fortior**is**	fortior**is**	fortior**is**
	dative	fortior**i**	fortior**i**	fortior**i**
	ablative	fortior**e**	fortior**e**	fortior**e**
plural	nominative	fortior**es**	fortior**es**	fortior**a**
	vocative	fortior**es**	fortior**es**	fortior**a**
	accusative	fortior**es**	fortior**es**	fortior**a**
	genitive	fortior**um**	fortior**um**	fortior**um**
	dative	fortior**ibus**	fortior**ibus**	fortior**ibus**
	ablative	fortior**ibus**	fortior**ibus**	fortior**ibus**

Note on *plus*

This is a bit of a one-off. As you can see, it does not end in *-or*. In the singular it exists as a noun, usually followed by a genitive. In the plural it exists as an adjective.

singular (noun)	nominative	plus		
	vocative	plus		
	accusative	plus		
	genitive	pluris		
	dative	(does not exist)		
	ablative	plure		

		masculine	feminine	neuter
plural (adjective)	nominative	plures	plures	plura
	vocative	plures	plures	plura
	accusative	plures	plures	plura
	genitive	plurium	plurium	plurium
	dative	pluribus	pluribus	pluribus
	ablative	pluribus	pluribus	pluribus

So: singular noun: more food = *plus cibi* more money = *plus pecuniae*
plural adjective: more soldiers = *plures milites* more wars = *plura bella*

Exercise 50.3

Translate into English:

1. non omnes magistri pessimi sunt.
2. magistri sapientissimi saepe sunt.
3. id iter non facile sed difficillimum erat.
4. milites Romani fortiores quam milites Graeci erant.
5. Iulius Caesar erat dux optimus.
6. ego plus pecuniae quam tu habeo.
7. tu es puella bona, sed ego melior sum.
8. plurimi milites oppidum oppugnaverunt.
9. villae Romanorum maximae erant.
10. Alexander Magnus miles melior quam Iulius Caesar erat.

Exercise 50.4

Translate into English:

1. maximae naves appropinquabant.
2. pueri peiores quam puellae sunt.
3. Romani milites meliores quam Graeci habebant.
4. plurimi cives urbem fortiter defendebant.
5. hortum pulchriorem numquam vidi.
6. heri ad urbem itinere faciliore venimus.
7. vulnus peius numquam acceperam.
8. puellae sapientiores quam pueri sunt.
9. Graeci meliora templa quam Romani aedificabant.
10. templa Graecorum pulchriora quam templa Romanorum erant.

Exercise 50.5

Translate into Latin:

1. The enemy were in very great danger.
2. I have never seen a bigger temple.
3. In the fields are very many horses.
4. We are carrying very many weapons.
5. The Greeks had more soldiers than the Trojans.

Exercise 50.6

Translate into English:

1. servus optimus

....

2. flumen altissimum

....

3. maxima turba

....

4. templum maius

....

5. libri difficillimi

....

6. villae pulcherrimae

....

7. plurimi captivi

....

8. caelum pulcherrimum

....

9. domina crudelissima

....

10. magister iratissimus

....

Exercise 50.7

Translate into English:

1. plurimi servi timebant et ex urbe effugiebant.

....

2. Romani minora templa quam Graeci aedificabant.

....

3. cives Graeci sapientiores quam cives Romani erant.

....

4. plurimas puellas pulcherrimas in urbe heri conspexi.

....

5. Troiani urbem contra hostes maxima virtute defendebant.

....

Chapter 51: The Story of Troy (Part 12)
possum

Exercise 51.1

The Greeks despair of taking Troy, but Ulysses (Odysseus) comes up with a plan.

1 diu Graeci urbem Troiam oppugnabant. <u>post</u> multos <u>annos</u> fessi erant. quamquam fortiter pugnaverant, urbem capere non <u>potuerant</u>.

   'quid faciemus?' <u>inquiunt</u>. 'hostes vincere non <u>possumus</u>. <u>num</u>
5 Troianos superabimus? muri Troiae maximi sunt. eos delere numquam <u>poterimus</u>. <u>hinc</u> discedere et ad Graeciam navigare <u>debemus</u>. tum <u>familias</u> nostras iterum videbimus.'

   Ulixes, miles audacissimus Graecorum, ubi ea verba audivit, iratus erat. magna voce clamavit:

10 'audite me, Graeci! <u>nolite</u> <u>stulti</u> esse! nos sapientiores quam Troiani sumus. Troiam mox capere <u>poterimus</u>. <u>hinc</u> discedere non <u>debetis</u>! consilium habeo. consilium optimum habeo. consilio meo urbem capiemus et delebimus. tum Troianos <u>punire</u> et Helenam <u>liberare</u> et eam ad Graeciam <u>reducere</u>
15 <u>poterimus</u>. equum <u>ligneum</u> maximum aedificate!'

post + acc. = after
annus, -i. m. = year
potuerant = they had been able
inquiunt = they said
possumus = we are able/can
num = surely... not...? *(introduces a question expecting the answer 'no')*
poterimus = we will be able
hinc = from here
debeo, -ere, debui (2) + infin. = have to, must, ought
familia, -ae f. = family

nolite + infin. = don't ...!
stultus, -a, -um = stupid
punio, -ire, punivi (4) = I punish
libero, -are, -avi (1) = I set free
reduco, -ere, -duxi (3) = I lead back
ligneus, -a, -um = wooden

(a copy of this passage in workbook format can be found on page 77.)

Exercise 51.2

1. From the passage above, give, in Latin, an example of:

   a. a verb in the pluperfect tense; ....

   b. a verb in the future tense; ....

   c. an imperative; ....

   d. a part of the pronoun *is ea id*. ....

2. **urbem** (line 1). Explain the connection between this word and the English word *suburban*.

   ....

   ....

   ....

3. **hostes** (line 4).

   a. In which case is this noun? ....

   b. Why is this case used? ....

4. **maximi** (line 5). This is a superlative adjective. Give the nominative masculine singular of its positive form. ....

5. **magna voce** (line 9). In what case is this expression? ....

Vocabulary Box 40a

debeo, -ere, debui (2) + infin.	I must, ought to
inquit/inquiunt	he/she/they say/said
libero, -are, -avi (1)	I set free
possum, posse, potui (irreg)	I am able, can
post + acc.	after
punio, -ire, punivi (4)	I punish
reduco, -ere, reduxi (3)	I lead back

Vocabulary Box 40b

after	post + acc.
I am able, can	possum, posse, potui (irreg)
I lead back	reduco, -ere, reduxi (3)
I must, ought to	debeo, -ere, debui (2) + infin.
I punish	punio, -ire, punivi (4)
I set free	libero, -are, -avi (1)
he/she/they say/said	inquit/inquiunt

Irregular verb: possum *I am able/can*

As you will see, there are strong similarities between this verb and the verb sum, *I am*.

	Present *can;* *am/is/are able*	Imperfect *could;* *was/were able*	Perfect *could;* *was/were able*	Future *will be able*	Pluperfect *had been able*
I	possum	poteram	potui	potero	potueram
You (sg)	potes	poteras	potuisti	poteris	potueras
He/She/It	potest	poterat	potuit	poterit	potuerat
We	possumus	poteramus	potuimus	poterimus	potueramus
You (pl)	potestis	poteratis	potuistis	poteritis	potueratis
They	possunt	poterant	potuerunt	poterunt	potuerant
Infinitive	posse *to be able*				

This verb will usually have an infinitive (*to*-word) in front of it, to complete the meaning.

Examples

puella **currere** non potest.
*The girl is not able **to run** = The girl cannot run.*

miles bene **pugnare** poterat.
*The soldier was able **to fight** well. = The soldier could fight well.*

The same construction applies to the verb debeo, *I must, ought to*:

Example

festinare debemus.
*We ought **to hurry** = We must hurry.*

Exercise 51.3

Translate into English:

1. legere possum.
2. effugere potest.
3. vincere possumus.
4. fugere poterant.
5. venire non possum.
6. currere non poteramus.
7. oppugnare potuerunt.
8. dormire non poteram.
9. laborare non possum.
10. videre non poterant.

Exercise 51.4

Translate into Latin:

1. We can sail.
2. You (sg) cannot laugh.
3. They could not escape.
4. We shall be able to come.
5. He can sing.
6. We could not fight.
7. I cannot wait.
8. They cannot write.
9. We could not decide.
10. You (pl) are not able to run.

Exercise 51.5

Translate into English:

1. nautae ad insulam navigare poterant.
2. Troianos vincere numquam poterimus.
3. milites urbem delere non poterant.
4. servi ex oppido effugere non poterant.
5. Romani tela iacere non poterant.
6. is rex bene regere non potest.
7. cives urbem bene defendere non poterant.
8. ad villam hodie venire non potuimus.
9. magistri omnia facere non possunt.
10. poeta librum longum scribere non poterit.

Exercise 51.6

Translate into Latin:

1. I can read.
2. We could not escape.
3. I shall not be able to work.
4. They could not attack.
5. You (pl) can depart.
6. They could not see.
7. He cannot reply.
8. She could not walk.
9. I can come.
10. They can enter.

Exercise 51.7

Translate into Latin:

1. The citizens will not be able to defend the town well against the enemy.
2. The leader could not prepare very big forces.
3. Who will be able to come to the temple tomorrow?
4. The master was not able to set free the slaves.
5. Our comrades were not able to run quickly.

Chapter 52: The Story of Troy (Part 13)
nonne and *num*; prohibitions

Exercise 52.1

The Trojans see the horse, but cannot decide what to do with it.

1 Graeci maximum equum <u>ligneum</u> fecerant. antequam in navibus discesserunt, plurimos milites in equum posuerunt et equum in <u>litore</u> prope urbem <u>reliquerunt</u>.

Troiani, ubi equum viderunt, ex urbe cucurrerunt et eum diu
5 spectaverunt. <u>unus</u> e Troianis 'Graeci' inquit 'discesserunt. <u>nonne</u> eos vicimus? is equus <u>donum</u> est. eum in <u>medium</u> urbem ducere debetis, cives!'

sed <u>senex</u> <u>quidam</u> magna voce '<u>num</u>' inquit 'equus <u>donum</u> est? Graeci <u>dona</u> numquam dant. Graeci <u>homines</u> <u>fallaces</u> sunt.
10 <u>nolite</u> equum in urbem ducere, cives! eum statim delere debemus!'

tandem Troiani equum in urbem <u>trahere</u> constituerunt. id consilium non sapiens fuit.

ligneus, -a, -um = wooden
litus, litoris n. = shore
relinquo, -ere, reliqui (3) = I abandon, leave behind

unus = one
nonne = surely…? *(introduces a question expecting the answer 'yes')*
donum, -i n. = gift
medius, -a, -um = middle of

senex, senis m. = old man
quidam = a certain
num = surely… not…? *(introduces a question expecting the answer 'no')*
homo, hominis m. = man, person; pl: people
fallax, fallacis = deceitful
nolite + infin. = Do not…!
traho, -ere, traxi (3) = I pull, drag

(a copy of this passage in workbook format can be found on page 78.)

Exercise 52.2

1. From the passage above, give, in Latin, an example of:

   a. a noun in the ablative case;

   ....

   b. a pronoun;

   ....

   c. an adverb;

   ....

   d. a noun in the vocative case.

   ....

2. **navibus** (line 2).

   a. In which case is this noun?

   b. Why is this case used?

   ....

3. **plurimos** (line 2). This is a superlative adjective. Give the nominative masculine singular of its positive and comparative forms.

   ....

3. **senex** (line 8). Explain the connection between this word and the English word *senility*.

   ....

   ....

   ....

```
┌─────────────────────────────────────────────────────────────┐
│                    Vocabulary Box 41a                        │
│                                                               │
│  donum, -i n.                     gift                        │
│  homo, hominis m.                 man, person; pl: people     │
│  medius, -a, -um                  middle of                   │
│  noli (sg) / nolite (pl) + infin. do not...!                  │
│  nonne?                           surely? (expecting a yes answer) │
│  num?                             surely not?(expecting a no answer) │
│  senex, senis m.                  old man                     │
└─────────────────────────────────────────────────────────────┘
```

```
┌─────────────────────────────────────────────────────────────┐
│                    Vocabulary Box 41b                        │
│                                                               │
│  do not...!                       noli (sg) / nolite (pl) + infin. │
│  gift                             donum, -i n.                │
│  man, person; pl: people          homo, hominis m.           │
│  middle of                        medius, -a, -um            │
│  old man                          senex, senis m.            │
│  surely? (expecting a yes answer) nonne?                     │
│  surely not?(expecting a no answer) num?                     │
└─────────────────────────────────────────────────────────────┘
```

Direct Questions

You have now met three ways of turning statements into questions.

1.   **-ne** on the end of the first word in a sentence. We met this at Level 1.
     This sort of question is simple – it expects the answer *yes* <u>or</u> *no*.
     So: puer laborat.   *The boy is working.*
        →   puer**ne** laborat?   *Is the boy working?*

2.   **nonne** (= non + ne) at the start of a sentence means that the answer *yes* is expected.
     So: **nonne** puer laborat?   *The boy <u>is</u> working, isn't he?*

3.   **num** at the start of a sentence means that the answer *no* is expected.
     So: **num** puer laborat?   *The boy <u>isn't</u> working, is he?*

In some dictionaries or listings (including this book!) you will see **nonne** translated as *surely?* and **num** translated as *surely not?* This gives a rough idea of what's going on, but these aren't really the actual meanings of these words. Using *surely* or *surely not* will often end up sounding like bad English. Try to avoid using *surely* or *surely not* if you can, and follow the pattern of the English examples given above by phrasing your translation accordingly. Here are some more:

nonne servus dominum necavit?   *The slave killed his master, didn't he?*
num servus dominum necavit?   *The slave didn't kill his master, did he?*

nonne miles bene pugnabat?   *The soldier was fighting well, wasn't he?*
num miles bene pugnabat?   *The soldier wasn't fighting well, was he?*

nonne bene dormies?   *You'll sleep well, won't you?*
num bene dormies?   *You won't sleep well, will you?*

Try to translate the exercises below without using the word *surely*.

Exercise 52.3

Translate into English:

1. num clamat?

   ....

2. nonne ridet?

   ....

3. pugnantne?

   ....

4. num pugnant?

   ....

5. nonne pugnant?

   ....

6. currebantne?

   ....

7. nonne currebant?

   ....

8. num currebant?

   ....

9. nonne festinavisti?

   ....

10. num effugerunt?

   ....

Exercise 52.4

Translate into English:

1. nonne miles bene pugnabat?

   ....

2. num miles bene pugnabat?

   ....

3. nonne Graeci multa arma collegerunt?

   ....

4. num templum aedificare difficile est?

   ....

5. nonne Hector fortissimus Troianorum erat?

   ....

Exercise 52.5

Translate into Latin:

1. They are shouting, aren't they?

   ....

2. We are not shouting, are we?

   ....

3. He was running, wasn't he?

   ....

4. He is a bad husband, isn't he?

   ....

5. We didn't fight well, did we?

   ....

6. You (sg) ran, didn't you?

   ....

7. They weren't laughing, were they?

   ....

8. The slaves escaped, didn't they?

   ....

9. It was easy, wasn't it?

   ....

10. He didn't say bad words, did he?

    ....

Exercise 52.6

Translate into Latin:

1. The Greeks will not capture the city, will they?

   ....

2. Surely the Trojans were defending the town well?

   ....

3. The Romans fought well in the battle, didn't they?

   ....

4. Not all teachers are very wise, are they?

   ....

5. The long journey will not be easy, will it?

   ....

Prohibitions

These are negative imperatives – commands telling someone <u>not</u> to do something. In English they start with the words *Do not...*

In Latin, singular prohibitions (telling one person not to do something) begin with the word **noli** (= *be unwilling...!*).

Plural prohibitions (telling more than one person not to do something) begin with the word **nolite** (= *be unwilling...!*).

The **noli/nolite** is followed by an infinitive (*to*-word). So:

noli currere, serve!   = *Be unwilling to run, slave!*   = *Do not run, slave!*   (singular imperative)
nolite currere, servi! = *Be unwilling to run, slaves!* = *Do not run, slaves!*   (plural imperative)

Reminder: the person being told not to do something will have a <u>vocative</u> case ending.

Exercise 52.7

Translate into English:

1. noli ridere, puer!
2. nolite ridere, pueri!
3. nolite oppugnare, milites!
4. nolite effugere, servi!
5. noli intrare, iuvenis!
6. nolite navigare, nautae!
7. noli discedere, mater.
8. nolite timere, comites!
9. noli cantare, domina!
10. nolite pugnare, pueri mali!

Exercise 52.8

Translate into English:

1. nolite oppidum oppugnare, milites!
2. nolite verba magistri audire, pueri!
3. noli in media via stare, puella!
4. noli servum liberare, domine!
5. nolite urbem contra Graecos defendere, cives!
6. noli librum longum scribere, liberte!
7. noli pueros malos laudare, magister!
8. nolite iter longum facere, amici!
9. nolite me hic relinquere, comites!
10. noli pecuniam patri tradere, iuvenis!

Exercise 52.9

Translate into Latin:

1. Do not fight, soldiers!
2. Do not approach, boy!
3. Do not run, girls.
4. Do not work, slaves!
5. Do not attack, friend!

Exercise 52.10

Translate into Latin:

1. Do not hurry, mother!
2. Do not reply, slave!
3. Do not play in the garden, girls!
4. Do not drink all the wine, boy!
5. Do not listen to bad teachers, boys!

Chapter 53: The Story of Troy (Part 14)
Cardinal numbers 1-20; personal and reflexive pronouns

Exercise 53.1

The fall of Troy.

1 Troiani equum in urbem <u>traxerunt</u>. laetissimi erant quod Graeci discesserant. laetissimi erant quod Graecos vicerant.

ea <u>nocte</u> igitur omnes cives multum cibi consumebant et multum vini bibebant. mox omnes Troiani dormiebant.

5 media <u>nocte</u> milites Graeci <u>qui</u> in equo erant de equo <u>silentio</u> <u>descenderunt</u>. subito ad Troianos <u>dormientes</u> magnis <u>clamoribus</u> ruerunt. Troiani <u>se</u> defendere non poterant, <u>nam</u> sua arma non habebant. Graeci multos Troianos hastis et gladiis occiderunt. mox Troiam <u>occupaverant</u>. <u>paucos</u> Troianos
10 <u>vivos</u> reliquerunt.

sic Graeci urbem Troiam post <u>decem</u> <u>annos</u> <u>dolo</u> ceperunt. maximam <u>partem</u> urbis deleverunt. Helenam ad <u>Graeciam</u> reducere iam poterant.

traho, -ere, traxi (3) = I pull, drag
nox, noctis f. = night
qui = who
silentio = in silence
descendo, -ere, descendi (3) = I climb down
dormientes = as they were sleeping
clamor, clamoris m. = shout
se = themselves
nam = for
occupo, -are, occupavi (1) = I seize
pauci, -ae, -a (pl) = few
vivus, -a, -um = alive
decem = ten
annus, -i m. = year
dolus, -i m. = trickery
pars, partis f. = part
Graecia, -ae f. = Greece

(a copy of this passage in workbook format can be found on page 79.)

Exercise 53.2

1. From the passage above, give, in Latin, an example of:

   a. a superlative adjective;
   ....
   b. a verb in the pluperfect tense;
   ....
   c. a noun in the ablative case;
   ....
   d. an adverb.
   ....

2. **urbem** (line 1).

   a. In which case is this noun?
   ....
   b. Why is this case used?
   ....

3. **erant** (line 5). For this verb, give:

   a. its person;
   ....
   b. its number;
   ....
   c. its tense;
   ....
   d. the first person singular of its present tense.
   ....

Vocabulary Box 42a	
clamor, clamoris m.	shout
nam	for
occupo, -are, occupavi (1)	I seize
pars, partis f.	part
pauci, -ae, -a (pl)	few
se	himself/herself/themselves
vivus, -a, -um	alive

Vocabulary Box 42b	
alive	vivus, -a, -um
few	pauci, -ae, -a (pl)
for	nam
himself/herself/themselves	se
part	pars, partis f.
I seize	occupo, -are, occupavi (1)
shout	clamor, clamoris m.

At Level 1 you met the cardinal numbers from 1 to 10. Here are the numbers upto 20.

Cardinal Numbers 1 – 20			
unus	one	undecim	eleven
duo	two	duodecim	twelve
tres	three	tredecim	thirteen
quattuor	four	quattuordecim	fourteen
quinque	five	quindecim	fifteen
sex	six	sedecim	sixteen
septem	seven	septendecim	seventeen
octo	eight	duodeviginti	eighteen
novem	nine	undeviginti	nineteen
decem	ten	viginti	twenty

Personal Pronouns

These are words which take the place of nouns, e.g. *I, you, he, she, it, we, they.* You met the nominative and accusative forms of these at Level 1. Here are the complete tables:

First Person Pronoun: *ego*

	singular		plural	
nominative	ego	*I*	nos	*we*
accusative	me	*me*	nos	*us*
genitive	mei	*of me/my*	nostrum	*of us/our*
dative	mihi	*to/for me*	nobis	*to/for us*
ablative	me	*(by) me*	nobis	*(by) us*
note:	mecum	*with me*	nobiscum	*with us*

Second Person Pronoun: *tu*

	singular		plural	
nominative	tu	*you*	vos	*you*
accusative	te	*you*	vos	*you*
genitive	tui	*of you/your*	vestrum	*of you/your*
dative	tibi	*to/for you*	vobis	*to/for you*
ablative	te	*(by) you*	vobis	*(by) you*
note:	tecum	*with you*	vobiscum	*with you*

Nominative pronouns can add emphasis, or reinforce a contrast:

Examples
You are bad; **I** am good.
*tu malus es; **ego** bonus sum.*

We are Greek; **you** are Roman.
***nos** Graeci sumus; **vos** Romani estis.*

I have been a good boy. (but others may not have been)
***ego** puer bonus fui.*

Exercise 53.3   *Translate into English:*

1. ego te non amo.
2. tu me non amas.
3. da mihi pecuniam, domine!
4. ego tibi pecuniam dare non cupio, serve!
5. tu ludebas; ego laborabam.
6. num vos nos amatis?
7. cur a me fugis, puella?
8. ego eam puellam amo.
9. ea puella me non amat.
10. amici mecum heri ludebant.

Exercise 53.4   *Translate into English:*

1. pueri, nobiscum ludete!
2. hostes contra nos pugnant.
3. pater pecuniam tibi dat.
4. dominus pecuniam vobis dabit, servi.
5. servi ad me festinant.
6. amici mecum ludunt.
7. ego donum tibi cras dabo.
8. magister dona nobis numquam dat.
9. pater donum mihi, tibi pecuniam dedit.
10. is magister te, non me, amat.

Exercise 53.5   *Translate into Latin:*

1. I am a Roman man; you are a Greek woman.
2. We are good; you (pl) are bad.
3. I will give money to you (sg).
4. He often gives gifts to us.
5. Play with me, friends!
6. We do not wish to play with you (sg).
7. That girl will never give me a present.
8. I want to come with you (pl).
9. He is doing it for us.
10. Come with us, mother!

Reflexive Pronouns

These are pronouns which reflect ('bend back') the action of the verb onto the subject. In other words, the subject (doer) of the verb is also the object (receiver) of the same verb.

Third Person Reflexive Pronoun: *se*

	singular		plural	
nominative		(cannot exist)		(cannot exist)
accusative	se	*himself/herself*	se	*themselves*
genitive	sui	*of himself/of herself*	sui	*of themselves*
dative	sibi	*to/for himself/herself*	sibi	*to/for themselves*
ablative	se	*(by) himself/herself*	se	*(by) themselves*
note:	secum	*with him/with her*	secum	*with them*

Summary of reflexive pronouns

	singular		plural	
1st person	me	*myself*	nos	*ourselves*
2nd person	te	*yourself*	vos	*yourselves*
3rd person	se	*himself/herself/itself*	se	*themselves*

Exercise 53.6

Translate into English:

1. is puer se amat.
2. Romani se necare constituerunt.
3. Troiani se defendere paraverunt.
4. ea puella se semper spectat.
5. dux milites iter secum facere iussit.
6. pueri sapientes se numquam laudant.
7. cives Troiani se fortiter defendebant.
8. miles se gladio suo vulneravit.
9. cives tristes hostibus se tradiderunt.
10. senex se necare cupiebat.

Exercise 53.7

Translate into Latin:

1. I do not want to kill myself.
2. I was looking at myself in the river.
3. That slave works for himself.
4. The father ordered his son to walk with him.
5. The slaves were fighting among themselves.
6. Boy, why are you always praising yourself?
7. They took the money for themselves.
8. Soldiers, why are you not defending yourselves?
9. Bad teachers often praise themselves.
10. Why are we not defending ourselves?

Reading Passages
in
Workbook Format

Exercise 39.1 (page 1)

*Discord, the goddess of arguments, gatecrashes
the wedding party of Peleus and the sea-nymph Thetis.*

1 olim in <u>monte Olympo</u> dei et deae <u>laetissimi</u> erant. cibum consumebant et vinum bibebant. <u>laetissimi</u> erant quod Peleus <u>Thetim</u> <u>in matrimonium ducebat</u>. Thetis dea erat. Peleus vir <u>mortalis</u> erat. dei deae<u>que</u> laeti erant. ridebant.

5 subito tamen Discordia, dea mala, intravit. <u>ceteri</u> dei, ubi Discordiam viderunt, non laeti erant. non iam ridebant. non ridebant quod Discordiam non amabant. clamaverunt:

'quid cupis, Discordia? cur hic stas? te non amamus. statim discede!'

10 Discordia <u>nuntiavit</u>:

'me audite, dei! me audite, deae! <u>donum</u> habeo. <u>donum</u> pulchrum habeo. hic est.'

deinde Discordia <u>pomum</u> <u>deposuit</u>. risit discessit<u>que</u>. dei deae<u>que</u> ad <u>pomum</u> <u>appropinquaverunt</u>. <u>pomum</u>
15 spectaverunt.

---

monte Olympo = Mount Olympus

laetissimus, -a, -um = very happy

Thetim *is the accusative of* Thetis

in matrimonium duco (3) = I marry

mortalis = mortal

-que = and (*before* the word it is attached to)

ceteri = the rest of

nuntio (1) = I announce

donum, -i n. = gift, present

pomum, -i n. = apple
deposuit = (she) put down
appropinquo (1) = I approach

....

....

....

....

....

....

....

....

....

....

....

....

....

....

Exercise 40.1 (page 3)

On Mount Olympus the three goddesses Juno, Minerva and Venus
argue over the golden apple.

1   dei deaeque in <u>monte</u> Olympo erant. <u>pomum</u> spectabant. <u>pomum</u>
    pulchrum erat. <u>pomum</u> <u>aureum</u> erat. <u>haec</u> verba in <u>pomo</u> erant: '<u>hoc</u>
    <u>pomum</u> <u>aureum</u> feminae <u>pulcherrimae</u> est.'

    Iuno regina deorum erat. <u>et</u> <u>soror</u> <u>et</u> <u>uxor</u> Iovis erat. dea Iuno <u>pomum</u>
5   spectavit. verba legit.

    'ego dea <u>pulcherrima</u> sum,' clamavit. '<u>pomum</u> igitur meum est.'
    dea Minerva <u>pomum</u> spectavit. verba legit.

    '<u>erras</u>, Iuno,' clamavit. '<u>pomum</u> meum est. <u>pomum</u> meum est quod
    ego <u>pulcherrima</u> sum.'

10   dea Venus <u>pomum</u> spectavit. verba legit.

    '<u>erratis</u>, deae. ego <u>pulcherrima</u> sum. <u>pomum</u> igitur meum est. <u>pomum</u>
    <u>mihi tradite</u>!'

    sic <u>tres</u> deae de <u>pomo</u> <u>aureo</u> <u>disputabant</u>. <u>omnes</u> <u>pomum</u> habere
    cupiebant. ad <u>Iovem</u> appropinquare igitur constituerunt. <u>Iuppiter</u> <u>et</u>
15   <u>pater et</u> <u>rex</u> deorum erat.

mons, montis m. = mountain
pomum, -i n. = apple
aureus, -a, -um = golden
haec = these
hoc = this
pulcherrimus, -a, -um = the
   most beautiful
et... et... = both... and...
soror = sister
uxor = wife
Iuppiter, Iovis m. = Jupiter

erro, -are, -avi (1) = I am
  wrong

mihi tradite! = hand over to
  me!
tres = three
disputo, -are, -avi (1) = I
  argue
omnes = (they) all
pater = father
rex = king

....

....

....

....

....

....

....

....

....

....

....

....

....

....

Exercise 41.1 (page 10)

Jupiter passes the buck to Paris, prince of Troy

1 <u>tres</u> deae, ubi ad <u>Iovem</u> venerunt, <u>haec</u> verba dixerunt:

'<u>Iuppiter</u>, <u>pomum</u> <u>aureum</u> nos <u>tres</u> deae cupimus. quis est <u>pulcherrima</u>? lege! lege <u>nunc</u>!'

<u>Iuppiter</u> non laetus erat. iram dearum timebat.

5 'deae,' respondit, 'vos <u>omnes</u> <u>pulcherrimae</u> estis. vos <u>omnes</u> <u>corpora</u> pulcherrima habetis. ego legere non <u>possum</u>. est iuvenis, Paris <u>nomine</u>. in <u>urbe</u> Troia habitat. feminas pulchras amat. Paris <u>pulcherrimam</u> <u>leget</u>. <u>Paridem</u> rogate!'

<u>tres</u> deae iratae erant. <u>Paridem</u> tamen rogare constituerunt. itaque
10 ad <u>Paridem</u> <u>ierunt</u>. <u>iter</u> non <u>longum</u> erat. mox igitur ad <u>Paridem</u> <u>advenerunt</u>. Paris, ubi <u>lucem</u> claram in caelo vidit, timebat. deae <u>Paridem</u> <u>salutaverunt</u> et <u>omnia</u> de <u>pomo</u> <u>aureo</u> <u>narraverunt</u>.

'<u>Iuppiter</u> nos ad te misit, Paris. te deam <u>pulcherrimam</u> legere iubet. lege <u>nunc</u>!'

tres = three
Iuppiter, Iovis m. = Jupiter
haec = these
pomum, -i n. = apple
aureus, -a, -um = golden
pulcherrimus, -a, -um = the most beautiful
nunc = now
omnes = all
corpora = bodies
possum = I am able, I can
iuvenis, iuvenis m. = young man
nomine = by name
urbs, urbis f. = city
leget = (he) will chose
Paris, Paridis m. = Paris
ierunt = (they) went
iter, itineris n. = journey
longus, -a, -um = long
advenio, -ire, -veni (4) = I arrive
lux, lucis f. = light
saluto, -are, -avi (1) = I greet
omnia = everything
narro, -are, -avi (1) = I tell

Exercise 42.1 (page 15)

The goddesses cheat.

1	Paris timebat. respondit tamen: 'omnes pulcherrimae estis, deae! nunc legere non possum. cras redite! cras constituam!'

deae Paridi 'cras redibimus,' clamaverunt, sed diu exspectare non cupimus.' iratae discesserunt.

5   secreto tamen Iuno ad Paridem appropinquavit. haec verba Paridi dixit:

'si mihi pomum trades, ego te virum potentissimum faciam.' postquam haec verba dixit, discessit.

Minerva quoque ad Paridem secreto appropinquavit. haec verba
10   Paridi dixit:

'si tu me leges, ego te virum sapientissimum faciam.' postquam haec verba dixit, discessit.

postea Venus quoque ad Paridem secreto appropinquavit. haec verba Paridi dixit:

15   'si tu me leges, ego tibi feminam pulcherrimam uxorem dabo.' deinde discessit.

Paris solus iam erat.

Vocabulary:

Paris, Paridis m. = Paris
omnes = all
pulcherrimus, -a, -um = very beautiful
possum = I am able, I can
cras = tomorrow
redibimus = we will come back
exspecto, -are, -avi (1) = I wait (for)
secreto = in secret
Iuno = Juno
haec = these
si = if
pomum, -i n. = apple
mihi = to me
potentissimus, -a, -um = the most powerful
faciam = I shall make

sapientissimus, -a, -um = the wisest

postea = later

uxorem = as your wife

....

....

....

....

....

....

....

....

....

....

....

....

....

....

Exercise 44.1 (page 21)

The goddesses cheat.

1 postero die tres deae ad Paridem iterum venerunt. ante Paridem steterunt. Paridi haec verba dixerunt:

'Pari, deam pulcherrimam nun legere debes.'

Paris, quamquam iram dearum timebat, clamavit:

5 'ego Venerem lego. Venus super omnes alias dea pulcherrima est.'

Venus, ubi verba Paridis audivit, risit. laeta erat. Iuno tamen et Minerva, propter verba Paridis, non riserunt. non laetae erant. iratae discesserunt.

Paris Venerem spectavit. 'ego,' inquit, 'te legi. mulierem
10 pulcherrimam uxorem cupio. ubi est?'

Venus Paridi respondit:

'mulier pulcherrima Helena est. in Graecia in oppido Sparta cum marito Menelao habitat. naviga ad Graeciam, cape Helenam, eam ad urbem Troiam reduc! sic mulier pulcherrima tua uxor erit.'

postero die = on the next day
Paris, Paridis m. = Paris
ante + acc. = before
haec = these
pulcherrimus, -a, -um = most beautiful
debeo, -ere, debui + infin. (2) = I must, have to
quamquam = although
Venus, Veneris f. = Venus
super omnes alias = above all others
Iuno = Juno
propter + acc. = because of

mulier, mulieris f. = woman
uxorem = as my wife

eam = her
reduco, -ere, -duxi (3) = I lead /take back

....
....
....
....
....
....
....
....
....
....
....
....
....
....

Exercise 45.1 (page 23)

Paris leaves Troy, goes to the Greek city of Sparta and kidnaps Menelaus' wife Helen.

1 Helena mulier pulchra et clara erat. in urbe Sparta cum marito, Menelao nomine, habitabat. Paris vir clarus erat. in urbe Troia habitabat. Troia erat urbs in Asia <u>sita</u>.

sita = situated

Paris ex urbe Troia ad urbem Spartam navigavit. ubi advenit, e <u>nave</u>
5 <u>descendit</u> et ad <u>regiam</u> festinavit. ibi puella Helena Paridem salutavit. vidit. Paris, ubi Helenam vidit, <u>eam</u> statim amavit.

navis, navis f. = ship
descendit = disembarked, got off
regia, -ae f. = palace
eam = her

Paris Helenae 'te amo', inquit, 'Helena. veni! ex Graecia navigabimus et ego te ad urbem Troiam ducam! festina!'

Paris Helenam ad <u>navem</u> duxit. deinde celeriter <u>fugerunt</u>. Paris et
10 Helena ad urbem Troiam navigaverunt. Paris laetus erat. Menelaus <u>autem</u>, maritus Helenae, non laetus sed <u>iratissimus</u> erat.

fugio, -ere, fugi (3½) = I flee
autem = however
iratissimus = very angry

Exercise 46.1 (page 26)

*Menelaus appeals for help from other cities in Greece,
and the combined Greek forces sail to Troy, where the fighting begins.*

1 Menelaus iratus erat quod Paris uxorem, Helenam nomine, ad urbem Troiam <u>duxerat</u>. Menelaus Paridem punire et Troiam delere cupiebat. <u>copias</u> igitur parare et bellum contra <u>Troianos</u> <u>gerere</u>
5 constituit.

> duxerat = had taken
> copiae, -arum f.pl. = troops, forces
> Troianus, -a, -um = Trojan
> gero, -ere, gessi (3) = wage, carry on

nuntios igitur ad <u>omnes</u> urbes Graeciae misit. auxilium Graecorum rogavit. Graeci, ubi verba nuntiorum audiverunt, <u>milites</u> et naves <u>collegerunt</u> et <u>eas</u> <u>copias</u> ad Menelaum <u>sine</u> <u>mora</u> miserunt.

> omnes = all
> miles, militis m. = soldier
> colligo, -ere, collegi (3) = I collect
> eas = those
> sine + abl. = without
> mora, -ae f. = delay

10 Menelaus, ubi copias Graecorum vidit, laetus erat. Graeci <u>milites</u> navesque paraverunt et trans mare ad urbem Troiam celeriter navigaverunt. sed ubi naves ad <u>litus</u> appropinquaverunt, <u>nemo</u> ex Graecis in terram <u>desilire</u> <u>primus</u> cupiebat.

> litus, -oris n. = shore
> nemo = noone
> desilire = to jump down
> primus = first
> descendo, -ere, -di (3) = I climb down, disembark
> ruo, -ere, rui (3) = charge

15 tandem Protesilaus, <u>miles</u> Graecus, <u>primus</u> in terram <u>descendit</u>. ubi <u>is</u> <u>descendit</u>, ceteri Graeci <u>descenderunt</u>. contra Troianos <u>ruerunt</u> et multos <u>eorum</u> <u>occiderunt</u>. Protesilaus <u>autem</u>, postquam multa vulnera <u>accepit</u>, <u>primus</u> Graecus <u>occisus est</u>.

> is = he
> eorum = of them
> occido, -ere, occidi (3) = I kill
> autem = however
> accipio, -ere, accepi (3½) = I receive
> occisus est = (he) was killed

....

....

....

....

....

....

....

....

....

....

....

....

....

Exercise 47.1 (page 31)

The Greeks realise that capturing Troy will not be a five-minute job.
The Greek warrior Achilles wants to take revenge on the Trojan Hector.

1 Protesilaus mortuus erat. Graeci contra muros Troiae ruerant. sub muris fortiter pugnaverant, sed frustra. non multos Troianos vulneraverant. urbem non ceperant. Agamemnon, frater Menelai, dux Graecorum erat. non laetus erat. haec verba militibus dixit:

5 'comites cari, hostes hodie non superavimus. muri Troiae alti et validi sunt. cives Troiani fortes sunt. muros urbis bene defendunt. castra ponite! bene dormite! cras contra hostes iterum pugnabimus. sine dubio bellum longum erit.'

diu copiae Graecorum muros Troiae oppugnaverunt. eos tamen
10 delere non poterant. rex Troiae Priamus erat. multos liberos claros habebat. inter eos erat Hector. is semper magna virtute pro Troianis pugnabat. numquam mortem timebat.

inter Graecos quoque erant multi milites fortes. Achilles autem fortissimus erat. amicum carum, Patroclum nomine, habebat.
15 quod Hector Patroclum in proelio occiderat, Achilles iratissimus erat. Hectorem necare magnopere cupiebat.

ruerant = had charged
mortuus, -a, -um = dead
sub + abl. = under
pugnaverant = had fought
frustra = in vain
vulneraverant = had wounded
ceperant = had captured
dux, ducis m. = leader
haec = these
comes, comitis m. = comrade
carus, -a, -um = dear
hostes, -ium m.pl. = enemy
civis, civis m. = citizen
fortes = brave
defendo, -ere, defendi (3) =
   I defend
castra, -orum n.pl. = camp
dubium, -i n. = doubt
poterant = they were able
liberi, -orum m.pl. = children
inter + acc. = between, among
quoque = also
virtus, virtutis m. = bravery
pro + abl. = for
mors, mortis f. = death
fortissimus = the bravest
occiderat = had killed
iratissimus = very angry

....

....

....

....

....

....

....

....

....

....

....

....

Exercise 48.1 (page 38)

Achilles, angry because of Patroclus' death, tells Hector he will kill him.
Hector is not impressed.

1   Achilles iratus erat quod Hector Patroclum occiderat. Hectorem
    igitur occidere cupiebat.

    olim Troiani contra Graecos prope urbem Troiam pugnabant.
    <u>omnes</u> fortiter pugnabant. <u>tum</u> subito Achilles Hectorem in
5   proelio <u>forte</u> <u>conspexit</u>. ubi eum vidit, ei clamavit:

    'audi me, Hector! ego sum Achilles, <u>fortissimus</u> Graecorum. tu
    vir <u>crudelis</u> es. quod tu Patroclum, amicum meum, occidisti, ego
    te occidam!'

    Hector, ubi verba Achillis audivit, ei respondit:

10 'audi verba mea, Achilles! laetus sum quod ego Patroclum,
    amicum tuum, occidi. ego te non timeo. tu me non terres! tu
    <u>fortis</u> non es. tu <u>audax</u> non es. tu <u>nobilis</u> non es! veni! pugna!
    <u>victoria</u> mihi non <u>difficilis</u> sed <u>facilis</u> erit. ego te mox <u>vincam</u>!'

omnes = everyone
tum = then
forte = by chance
conspicio, -ere, conspexi,
    conspectum (3 ½) = I catch
    sight of
fortissimus = the bravest
crudelis = cruel

fortis = brave
audax = bold, daring
nobilis = noble
victoria, -ae f. = victoria
difficilis = difficult
facilis = easy
vinco, -ere, vici (3) = conquer

....

....

....

....

....

....

....

....

....

....

....

....

....

....

....

Exercise 49.1 (page 42)

Achilles fights Hector.

1 Achilles Hectorem spectabat. Hector Achillem spectabat. Hector vir fortis et <u>audax</u> erat. Achilles tamen <u>fortior</u> et <u>audacior</u> <u>quam</u> Hector erat.

   subito Hector <u>telum</u> suum iecit. <u>telum</u> ad Achillem <u>celeriter</u>
5 <u>volavit</u>. in scuto tamen Achillis <u>haesit</u>. eum non <u>vulneraverat</u>. Achilles, ubi <u>hoc</u> vidit, risit. deinde, <u>antequam</u> suum <u>telum</u> iecit, Hectori verba crudelia magna <u>voce</u> dixit: 'tu me non occidisti, Hector. <u>nemo</u> <u>fortior</u> est <u>quam</u> ego. ego sum <u>fortissimus</u> omnium Graecorum. <u>nihil</u> timeo.'

10 ubi <u>haec</u> verba dixit, sine mora <u>telum</u> ad Hectorem iecit. <u>telum</u> ad Hectorem <u>celeriter</u> <u>volavit</u> et in corpore eius <u>haesit</u>. Hector ad terram <u>cecidit</u> mortuus. Achilles <u>laetissimus</u> erat. risit.

audax = bold, daring
fortior = braver
audacior = more daring
quam = than
telum, -i n. = spear
celeriter = quickly
volo, -are, volavi (1) = I fly
haereo, -ere, haesi (2) = I stick
vulnero, -are, -avi (1) = I wound
hoc = this
antequam = before
vox, vocis f. = voice
nemo = noone
fortissimus = the bravest
nihil = nothing
haec = these
cado, -ere, cecidi (3) = I fall
laetissimus = very happy

....

....

....

....

....

....

....

....

....

....

....

....

....

....

....

....

....

....

Exercise 50.1 (page 46)

Achilles mistreats Hector's body. Hector's brother, Paris, takes revenge.

1 nemo <u>crudelior</u> quam Achilles erat. is corpus Hectoris <u>currui</u> suo <u>pedibus</u> <u>vinxit</u>. deinde <u>currum</u> <u>circum</u> muros Troiae <u>egit</u>, corpus Hectoris <u>trahens</u>. propter id omnes cives Troiani <u>tristissimi</u> et <u>iratissimi</u> erant.

5 Paris frater Hectoris erat. iratus quod Achilles Hectorem occiderat, arma cepit, ex urbe cucurrit, in proelium ruit. Achillem statim necare cupiebat. mox eum <u>invenit</u>. tum ei clamavit:

'Achilles, vir <u>pessimus</u> es. nemo <u>peior</u> est quam tu.
10 Hectorem, fratrem meum, occidisti. ego tamen miles <u>melior</u> sum quam tu. numquam <u>effugies</u>. nemo te <u>servare</u> <u>poterit</u>. te nunc occidam.'

Paris <u>telum</u> in Achillem misit. <u>telum</u> in <u>calce</u> Achillis <u>haesit</u>. Achilles ad terram mortuus <u>cecidit</u>.

crudelior = more cruel
currui = dative of currus = chariot
pes, pedis m. = foot
vincio, -ire, vinxi (4) = I tie
circum + acc. = around
trahens = dragging
tristissimus, a -um = very sad
iratissimus, -a, -um = very angry

invenio, -ire, -veni (4) = I find

pessimus, -a, -um = very wicked
peior, peioris = more wicked
melior, melioris = better
effugio, -ere, effugi (3½) =
  I escape
servo, -are, -avi (1) = I save
poterit = will be able
calx, calcis f. = heel
haereo, -ere, haesi (2) = I stick
cado, -ere, cecidi (3) = I fall, drop

....
....
....
....
....
....
....
....
....
....
....
....
....
....
....
....

Exercise 51.1 (page 51)

The Greeks despair of taking Troy, but Ulysses (Odysseus) comes up with a plan.

1　diu Graeci urbem Troiam oppugnabant. <u>post</u> multos <u>annos</u> fessi erant. quamquam fortiter pugnaverant, urbem capere non <u>potuerant</u>.

　　'quid faciemus?' <u>inquiunt</u>. 'hostes vincere non <u>possumus</u>. <u>num</u>
5　Troianos superabimus? muri Troiae maximi sunt. eos delere numquam <u>poterimus</u>. <u>hinc</u> discedere et ad Graeciam navigare <u>debemus</u>. tum <u>familias</u> nostras iterum videbimus.'

　　Ulixes, miles audacissimus Graecorum, ubi ea verba audivit, iratus erat. magna voce clamavit:

10　'audite me, Graeci! <u>nolite</u> <u>stulti</u> esse! nos sapientiores quam Troiani sumus. Troiam mox capere <u>poterimus</u>. <u>hinc</u> discedere non <u>debetis</u>! consilium habeo. consilium optimum habeo. consilio meo urbem capiemus et delebimus. tum Troianos <u>punire</u> et Helenam <u>liberare</u> et eam ad Graeciam <u>reducere</u>
15　<u>poterimus</u>. equum <u>ligneum</u> maximum aedificate!'

post + acc. = after
annus, -i. m. = year
potuerant = they had been able
inquiunt = they said
possumus = we are able/can
num = surely... not…? *(introduces a question expecting the answer 'no')*
poterimus = we will be able
hinc = from here
debeo, -ere, debui (2) + infin. = have to, must, ought
familia, -ae f. = family

nolite + infin. = don't …!
stultus, -a, -um = stupid
punio, -ire, punivi (4) = I punish
libero, -are, -avi (1) = I set free
reduco, -ere, -duxi (3) = I lead back
ligneus, -a, -um = wooden

....
....
....
....
....
....
....
....
....
....
....
....
....
....
....
....
....

Exercise 52.1 (page 54)

The Trojans see the horse, but cannot decide what to do with it.

1 Graeci maximum equum <u>ligneum</u> fecerant. antequam in navibus discesserunt, plurimos milites in equum posuerunt et equum in <u>litore</u> prope urbem <u>reliquerunt</u>.

Troiani, ubi equum viderunt, ex urbe cucurrerunt et eum diu
5 spectaverunt. <u>unus</u> e Troianis 'Graeci' inquit 'discesserunt. <u>nonne</u> eos vicimus? is equus <u>donum</u> est. eum in <u>medium</u> urbem ducere debetis, cives!'

sed <u>senex</u> <u>quidam</u> magna voce '<u>num</u>' inquit 'equus <u>donum</u> est? Graeci <u>dona</u> numquam dant. Graeci <u>homines</u> <u>fallaces</u> sunt.
10 <u>nolite</u> equum in urbem ducere, cives! eum statim delere debemus!'

tandem Troiani equum in urbem <u>trahere</u> constituerunt. id consilium non sapiens fuit.

ligneus, -a, -um = wooden
litus, litoris n. = shore
relinquo, -ere, reliqui (3) = I abandon, leave behind

ununs = one
nonne = surely...? *(introduces a question expecting the answer 'yes')*
donum, -i n. = gift
medius, -a, -um = middle of

senex, senis m. = old man
quidam = a certain
num = surely... not...? *(introduces a question expecting the answer 'no')*
homo, hominis m. = man, person; pl: people
fallax, fallacis = deceitful
nolite + infin. = Do not...!
traho, -ere, traxi (3) = I pull, drag

....
....
....
....
....
....
....
....
....
....
....
....
....
....
....
....

Exercise 53.1 (page 59)

The fall of Troy.

1   Troiani equum in urbem <u>traxerunt</u>. laetissimi erant quod Graeci discesserant. laetissimi erant quod Graecos vicerant.

    ea <u>nocte</u> igitur omnes cives multum cibi consumebant et multum vini bibebant. mox omnes Troiani dormiebant.

5   media <u>nocte</u> milites Graeci, <u>qui</u> in equo erant, de equo <u>silentio</u> <u>descenderunt</u>. subito ad Troianos <u>dormientes</u> magnis <u>clamoribus</u> ruerunt. Troiani <u>se</u> defendere non poterant, <u>nam</u> sua arma non habebant. Graeci multos Troianos hastis et gladiis occiderunt. mox Troiam <u>occupaverant</u>. <u>paucos</u> Troianos
10 <u>vivos</u> reliquerunt.

    sic Graeci urbem Troiam post <u>decem</u> <u>annos</u> <u>dolo</u> ceperunt. maximam <u>partem</u> urbis deleverunt. Helenam ad <u>Graeciam</u> reducere iam poterant.

traho, -ere, traxi (3) = I pull, drag
nox, noctis f. = night
qui = who
silentio = in silence
descendo, -ere, descendi (3) = I climb down
dormientes = as they were sleeping
clamor, clamoris m. = shout
se = themselves
nam = for
occupo, -are, occupavi (1) = I seize
pauci, -ae, -a (pl) = few
vivus, -a, -um = alive
decem = ten
annus, -i m. = year
dolus, -i m. = trickery
pars, partis f. = part
Graecia, -ae f. = Greece

....
....
....
....
....
....
....
....
....
....
....
....
....
....
....
....
....
....

Reference Section

List 1:   Vocabulary Checklist   82

List 2:   Principal Parts Checklist   85

English-into-Latin Sentences Revision

List 3a: Latin only checklist   87

List 3b: English-Latin alphabetical   88

List 3c: English-Latin by word-type   89

List 3d: English-Latin word groupings   90

Grammar Reference

List 4a: Grammatical terms   91

List 4b: Nouns   92

List 4c: Adjectives   94

List 5:   Pronouns   98

List 6:   Prepositions   100

List 7:   Verbs   102

List 8:   Syntax   104

List 9:   Cardinal numbers   107

Level 1 Revision Check-list   108

Level 2 Revision Check-list   109

List 10:   English-Latin Quick Reference   110

List 11:   Latin-English Quick Reference   115

List 1: Vocabulary Checklist

Adjectives

1.	altus	high, deep
2.	audax	bold, daring
3.	bonus	good
4.	carus	dear
5.	ceteri	the rest of
6.	clarus	clear, bright, famous
7.	crudelis	cruel
8.	difficilis	difficult
9.	facilis	easy
10.	felix	lucky, fortunate
11.	fessus	tired
12.	fortis	brave
13.	Graecus	Greek
14.	ingens	huge
15.	iratus	angry
16.	laetus	happy
17.	longus	long
18.	magnus	big, great
19.	malus	bad, evil, wicked
20.	meus	my
21.	miser	miserable
22.	mortuus	dead
23.	multus	much, many
24.	nobilis	noble
25.	noster	our
26.	notus	well known
27.	novus	new
28.	omnis	all, every
29.	parvus	small
30.	pauci	few
31.	pulcher	beautiful, handsome
32.	Romanus	Roman
33.	sacer	sacred
34.	saevus	savage
35.	sapiens	wise
36.	solus	alone
37.	suus	his/her/their own
38.	tristis	sad
39.	Troianus	Trojan
40.	tutus	safe
41.	tuus	your (sg)
42.	validus	strong
43.	vester	your (pl)
44.	vivus	alive

Adverbs

45.	bene	well
46.	celeriter	quickly
47.	cras	tomorrow
48.	diu	for a long time
49.	forte	by chance
50.	fortiter	bravely
51.	frustra	in vain
52.	heri	yesterday
53.	hic	here
54.	hodie	today
55.	iam	now, already
56.	ibi	there
57.	iterum	again
58.	magnopere	greatly
59.	medius	middle of
60.	mox	soon
61.	non	not
62.	numquam	never
63.	nunc	now, later
64.	olim	one day, once upon a time
65.	postea	afterwards
66.	quam	than
67.	saepe	often
68.	semper	always
69.	sic	in this way, thus
70.	statim	immediately
71.	subito	suddenly
72.	tandem	finally
73.	tum	then

Conjunctions

74.	autem	however
75.	antequam	before
76.	deinde	then, next
77.	et	and
78.	et ... et ...	both ... and ...
79.	etiam	also, even
80.	igitur	therefore
81.	itaque	and so
82.	nam	for
83.	postquam	after
84.	quamquam	although
85.	-que	and
86.	quod	because
87.	quoque	also
88.	sed	but
89.	tamen	however
90.	ubi	when

Interrogatives (question words)

91.	cur?	why?
92.	-ne	(indicates a question)
93.	nonne?	surely? (expecting 'yes')
94.	num?	surely … not? (expecting 'no')
95.	quid?	what?
96.	quis?	who?
97.	ubi?	where?

Nouns

98.	ancilla	slave girl, maidservant
99.	aqua	water
100.	cena	dinner
101.	copiae	troops, forces
102.	dea	goddess
103.	domina	mistress
104.	epistula	letter
105.	femina	woman
106.	filia	daughter
107.	Graecia	Greece
108.	hasta	spear
109.	insula	island
110.	ira	anger
111.	mora	delay
112.	patria	homeland
113.	pecunia	money
114.	puella	girl
115.	regina	queen
116.	Roma	Rome
117.	sagitta	arrow
118.	silva	wood
119.	terra	land
120.	Troia	Troy
121.	turba	crowd
122.	unda	wave
123.	via	road
124.	villa	villa
125.	agricola	farmer
126.	incola	inhabitant
127.	nauta	sailor
128.	poeta	poet
129.	ager	field
130.	amicus	friend
131.	captivus	prisoner
132.	cibus	food
133.	deus	god
134.	dominus	master
135.	equus	horse
136.	filius	son
137.	gladius	sword
138.	hortus	garden
139.	liber	book
140.	liberi	children
141.	libertus	freedman, ex-slave
142.	locus	place
143.	magister	teacher, master
144.	maritus	husband
145.	murus	wall
146.	nuntius	messenger
147.	puer	boy
148.	servus	slave
149.	socius	ally
150.	ventus	wind
151.	vir	man
152.	arma	weapons
153.	aurum	gold
154.	auxilium	help
155.	bellum	war
156.	caelum	sky
157.	consilium	plan
158.	donum	gift
159.	forum	forum, market place
160.	oppidum	town
161.	periculum	danger
162.	proelium	battle
163.	scutum	shield
164.	templum	temple
165.	verbum	word
166.	vinum	wine
167.	civis	citizen
168.	clamor	shout
169.	comes	companion
170.	dux	leader
171.	frater	brother
172.	homo	man, person
173.	hostes	enemy
174.	iuvenis	young man
175.	lux	light
176.	mater	mother
177.	miles	soldier
178.	mons	mountain
179.	mors	death
180.	mulier	woman
181.	navis	ship
182.	parens	parent
183.	pars	part
184.	pater	father
185.	rex	king
186.	senex	old man
187.	soror	sister
188.	urbs	city
189.	uxor	wife
190.	virtus	bravery
191.	vox	voice
192.	corpus	body
193.	flumen	river
194.	iter	journey
195.	mare	sea

196. nomen	name	243. se	him/herself, themselves
197. vulnus	wound	244. tu	you (sg)
198. nemo	noone	245. vos	you (pl)
199. nihil	nothing		

Numbers

200. unus	one
201. duo	two
202. tres	three
203. quattuor	four
204. quinque	five
205. sex	six
206. septem	seven
207. octo	eight
208. novem	nine
209. decem	ten
210. undecim	eleven
211. duodecim	twelve
212. tredecim	thirteen
213. quattuordecim	fourteen
214. quindecim	fifteen
215. sedecim	sixteen
216. septendecim	seventeen
217. duodeviginti	eighteen
218. undeviginti	nineteen
219. viginti	twenty

Verbs (1)

246. aedifico	build
247. ambulo	walk
248. amo	love, like
249. appropinquo	approach
250. canto	sing
251. clamo	shout
252. do	give
253. erro	wander, be wrong
254. exspecto	wait for
255. festino	hurry
256. habito	live
257. intro	enter
258. laboro	work
259. laudo	praise
260. libero	set free
261. narro	tell
262. navigo	sail
263. neco	kill
264. nuntio	announce
265. occupo	seize
266. oppugno	attack
267. paro	prepare
268. porto	carry
269. pugno	fight
270. rogo	ask, ask for
271. saluto	greet
272. servo	save
273. specto	watch, look at
274. sto	stand
275. supero	overcome
276. voco	call
277. vulnero	wound

Prepositions

220. a/ab + abl	away from
221. cum + abl	with
222. de + abl	down from, about
223. e/ex + abl	out of
224. pro + abl	for
225. sine + abl	without
226. sub + abl	under
227. ad + acc	to, towards
228. ante + acc	before
229. circum + acc	around
230. contra + acc	against
231. inter + acc	between, among
232. per + acc	through, along
233. post + acc	after
234. prope + acc	near
235. propter + acc	on account of
236. super + acc	above
237. trans + acc	across
238. in + abl	in, on
239. in + acc	into

Verbs (2)

278. debeo	have to, must
279. deleo	destroy
280. habeo	have
281. iubeo	order
282. maneo	stay
283. moneo	warn
284. moveo	move
285. respondeo	reply
286. rideo	laugh
287. teneo	hold
288. terreo	frighten
289. timeo	fear
290. video	see

Pronouns

240. ego	I
241. is	he, she, it
242. nos	we

Verbs (3)

291.	bibo	drink
292.	colligo	collect
293.	constituo	decide
294.	consumo	eat
295.	curro	run
296.	defendo	defend
297.	dico	say
298.	discedo	depart
299.	duco	lead
300.	gero	wage, carry on
301.	lego	read; choose
302.	ludo	play
303.	mitto	send
304.	occido	kill
305.	ostendo	show
306.	pono	put
307.	reduco	lead back
308.	rego	rule
309.	ruo	charge
310.	scribo	write
311.	trado	hand over
312.	vinco	conquer

Verbs (3½)

313.	accipio	receive
314.	capio	take, capture
315.	conspicio	catch sight of
316.	cupio	want
317.	effugio	escape
318.	facio	do, make
319.	fugio	flee
320.	iacio	throw

Verbs (4)

321.	advenio	arrive
322.	audio	hear, listen to
323.	dormio	sleep
324.	invenio	find
325.	punio	punish
326.	venio	come

Verbs (irreg)

327.	absum	be away
328.	adsum	be present
329.	inquit/inquiunt	he/they say/said
330.	noli/nolite	do not ...!
331.	possum	am able, can
332.	sum	be

List 2: Principal Parts Checklist

present tense	infinitive	perfect tense
e.g. I build	to build	I built/I have built

First Conjugation

246.	aedifico	aedificare	aedificavi	build
247.	ambulo	ambulare	ambulavi	walk
248.	amo	amare	amavi	love, like
249.	appropinquo	-quare	-quavi	approach
250.	canto	cantare	cantavi	sing
251.	clamo	clamare	clamavi	shout
252.	do	dare	dedi	give
253.	erro	errare	erravi	wander, be wrong
254.	exspecto	exspectare	exspectavi	wait for
255.	festino	festinare	festinavi	hurry
256.	habito	habitare	habitavi	live
257.	intro	intrare	intravi	enter
258.	laboro	laborare	laboravi	work
259.	laudo	laudare	laudavi	praise
260.	libero	liberare	liberavi	set free
261.	narro	narrare	narravi	tell
262.	navigo	navigare	navigavi	sail
263.	neco	necare	necavi	kill
264.	nuntio	nuntiare	nuntiavi	announce
265.	occupo	occupare	occupavi	seize
266.	oppugno	oppugnare	oppugnavi	attack

267. paro	parare	paravi	prepare
268. porto	portare	portavi	carry
269. pugno	pugnare	pugnavi	fight
270. rogo	rogare	rogavi	ask, ask for
271. saluto	salutare	salutavi	greet
272. servo	servare	servavi	save
273. specto	spectare	spectavi	watch, look at
274. sto	stare	steti	stand
275. supero	superare	superavi	overcome
276. voco	vocare	vocavi	call
277. vulnero	vulnerare	vulneravi	wound

Second Conjugation

278. debeo	debere	debui	have to, must
279. deleo	delere	delevi	destroy
280. habeo	habere	habui	have
281. iubeo	iubere	iussi	order
282. maneo	manere	mansi	stay
283. moneo	monere	monui	warn
284. moveo	movere	movi	move
285. respondeo	respondere	respondi	reply
286. rideo	ridere	risi	laugh
287. teneo	tenere	tenui	hold
288. terreo	terrere	terrui	frighten
289. timeo	timere	timui	fear
290. video	videre	vidi	see

Third Conjugation

291. bibo	bibere	bibi	drink
292. colligo	colligere	collegi	collect
293. constituo	constituere	constitui	decide
294. consumo	consumere	consumpsi	eat
295. curro	currere	cucurri	run
296. defendo	defendere	defendi	defend
297. dico	dicere	dixi	say
298. discedo	discedere	discessi	depart
299. duco	ducere	duxi	lead
300. gero	gerere	gessi	wage, carry on
301. lego	legere	legi	read; choose
302. ludo	ludere	lusi	play
303. mitto	mittere	misi	send
304. occido	occidere	occidi	kill
305. ostendo	ostendere	ostendi	show
306. pono	ponere	posui	put
307. reduco	reducere	reduxi	lead back
308. rego	regere	rexi	rule
309. ruo	ruere	rui	charge
310. scribo	scribere	scripsi	write
311. trado	tradere	tradidi	hand over
312. vinco	vincere	vici	conquer

Mixed Conjugation (3½)

313. accipio	accipere	accepi	receive
314. capio	capere	cepi	take, capture
315. conspicio	conspicere	conspexi	catch sight of
316. cupio	cupere	cupivi	want
317. effugio	effugere	effugi	escape
318. facio	facere	feci	do, make
319. fugio	fugere	fugi	flee
320. iacio	iacere	ieci	throw

Fourth Conjugation

321. advenio			
322. audio	audire	audivi	hear, listen to
323. dormio	dormire	dormivi	sleep
324. invenio	invenire	inveni	find
325. punio	punire	punivi	punish
326. venio	venire	veni	come

Irregulars

327. absum	abesse	afui	be away
328. adsum	adesse	adfui	be present
329. inquit/inquiunt			he/they say/said
330. noli/nolite			do not … !
331. possum	posse	potui	be able
332. sum	esse	fui	be

List 3: English-into-Latin Sentences Revision

List 3a : Latin only checklist

a/ab	femina	murus	saevus
ad	filius	nauta	semper
aedifico	gladius	neco	servus
amicus	habeo	non	specto
amo	hasta	numquam	statim
ancilla	in + abl	oppidum	sum
bonus	in + acc	paro	tamen
cena	intro	parvus	tandem
clamo	laetus	pecunia	templum
clarus	laudo	porto	timeo
cum	liber	prope	via
deleo	magister	puella	video
deus	magnus	puer	villa
dominus	malus	pugno	vinum
e/ex	miser	pulcher	vir
epistula	moneo	regina	voco
equus	mox	Romanus	
et	multus	saepe	

List 3b: English-Latin alphabetical checklist

always	semper	maidservant	ancilla, -ae f.
and	et	man	vir, viri m.
at last	tandem	many	multus, -a, -um
away from	a/ab + abl.	master	dominus, -i m; magister, -tri m.
bad	malus, -a, -um	meal	cena, -ae f.
be	sum, esse, fui (irreg)	miserable	miser, -era, -erum
be afraid of	timeo, -ere, -ui (2)	much	multus, -a, -um
beautiful	pulcher, -chra, -chrum	near	prope + acc.
big	magnus, -a, -um	never	numquam
book	liber, libri m.	not	non
boy	puer, pueri m.	often	saepe
bright	clarus, -a, -um	on	in + abl.
build	aedifico, -are, -avi (1)	onto	in + acc.
call	voco, -are, -avi (1)	out of	e/ex + abl.
carry	porto, -are, -avi (1)	praise	laudo, -are, -avi (1)
clear	clarus, -a, -um	prepare	paro, -are, -avi (1)
cruel	saevus, -a, -um	queen	regina, -ae f.
destroy	deleo, -ere, delevi (2)	road	via, -ae f.
dinner	cena, -ae f.	Roman	Romanus, -a, -um
enter	intro, -are, -avi (1)	see	video, -ere, vidi (2)
evil	malus, -a, -um	sailor	nauta, -ae m.
famous	clarus, -a, -um	savage	saevus, -a, -um
fear	timeo, -ere, timui (2)	slave	servus, -i m.
fight	pugno, -are, -avi (1)	slavegirl	ancilla, -ae f.
finally	tandem	small	parvus, -a, -um
friend	amicus, -i m.	son	filius, -i m.
from	a/ab + abl.	soon	mox
girl	puella, -ae f.	spear	hasta, -ae f.
god	deus, -i m.	street	via, -ae f.
good	bonus, -a, -um	sword	gladius, -i m.
great	magnus, -a, -um	teacher	magister, -tri m.
handsome	pulcher, -chra, -chrum	temple	templum, -i n.
happy	laetus, -a, -um	to	ad + acc.
have	habeo, -ere, -ui (2)	towards	ad + acc.
horse	equus, -i m.	town	oppidum, -i n.
house	villa, -ae f.	unhappy	miser, -era, -erum
however	tamen	villa	villa, -ae f.
immediately	statim	wall	murus, -i m.
in	in + abl.	warn	moneo, -ere, -ui (2)
into	in + acc.	watch	specto, -are, -avi (1)
kill	neco, -are, -avi (1)	wicked	malus, -a, -um
large	magnus, -a, -um	wine	vinum, -i n.
letter	epistula, -ae f.	with	cum + abl.
like	amo, -are, -avi (1)	woman	femina, -ae f.
little	parvus, -a, -um	wretched	miser, -era, -erum
look at	specto, -are, -avi (1)		
love	amo , -are, -avi (1)		

List 3c: English-Latin by word-type

Adjectives

1. bad — malus, -a, -um
2. beautiful — pulcher, -chra, -chrum
3. big — magnus, -a, -um
4. bright — clarus, -a, -um
5. clear — clarus, -a, -um
6. cruel — saevus, -a, -um
7. evil — malus, -a, -um
8. famous — clarus, -a, -um
9. good — bonus, -a, -um
10. great — magnus, -a, -um
11. handsome — pulcher, -chra, -chrum
12. happy — laetus, -a, -um
13. large — magnus, -a, -um
14. little — parvus, -a, -um
15. many — multus, -a, -um
16. miserable — miser, -era, -erum
17. much — multus, -a, -um
18. Roman — Romanus, -a, -um
19. savage — saevus, -a, -um
20. small — parvus, -a, -um
21. unhappy — miser, -era, -erum
22. wicked — malus, -a, -um
23. wretched — miser, -era, -erum

Nouns

24. book — liber, libri m.
25. boy — puer, -i m.
26. dinner — cena, -ae f.
27. friend — amicus, -i m.
28. girl — puella, -ae f.
29. god — deus, -i m.
30. horse — equus, -i m.
31. letter — epistula, -ae f.
32. maidservant — ancilla, -ae f.
33. man — vir, viri m.
34. master — dominus, -i m.; magister, -tri m.
35. meal — cena, -ae f.
36. money — pecunia, -ae f.
37. queen — regina, -ae f.
38. road — via, -ae f.
39. sailor — nauta, -ae m.
40. slave — servus, -i m.
41. slavegirl — ancilla, -ae f.
42. son — filius, -i m.
43. spear — hasta, ae f.
44. street — via, -ae f.
45. sword — gladius, -i m.
46. teacher — magister, -tri m.
47. temple — templum, -i n.
48. town — oppidum, -i n.
49. villa — villa, -ae f.
50. wall — murus, -i m.
51. wine — vinum, -i n.
52. woman — femina, -ae f.

Prepositions

53. away from — a/ab + abl.
54. in, on — in + abl.
55. into, onto — in + abl.
56. near — prope + acc.
57. out of — e/ex + abl.
58. to, towards — ad + acc.
59. with — cum + abl.

Verbs

60. be — sum, esse, fui (irreg)
61. build — aedifico, -are, -avi (1)
62. call — voco, -are, -avi (1)
63. carry — porto, -are, -avi (1)
64. destroy — deleo, -ere delevi (2)
65. enter — intro, -are, -avi (1)
66. fear — timeo, -ere -ui (2)
67. fight — pugno, -are, -avi (1)
68. have — habeo, -ere, -ui (2)
69. kill — neco, -are, -avi (1)
70. like — amo, -are, -avi (1)
71. look at — specto, -are, -avi (1)
72. love — amo, -are, -avi (1)
73. praise — laudo, -are, -avi (1)
74. prepare — paro, -are, -avi (1)
75. see — video, -ere vidi (2)
76. shout — clamo, -are, -avi (1)
77. walk — ambulo, -are, -avi (1)
78. warn — moneo, -ere, -ui (2)
79. watch — specto, -are, -avi (1)

Others

80. always — semper
81. and — et
82. at last — tandem
83. at once — statim
84. finally — tandem
85. however — tamen
86. immediately — statim
87. never — numquam
88. not — non
89. often — saepe
90. soon — mox

List 3d: English-Latin word groupings

Adjectives

1. bad — malus, -a, -um
2. big — magnus, -a, -um
3. bright — clarus, -a, -um
4. clear — clarus, -a, -um
5. cruel — saevus, -a, -um
6. evil — malus, -a, -um
7. famous — clarus, -a, -um
8. good — bonus, -a, -um
9. great — magnus, -a, -um
10. happy — laetus, -a, -um
11. large — magnus, -a, -um
12. little — parvus, -a, -um
13. many — multi, -ae, -a
14. much — multus, -a, -um
15. Roman — Romanus, -a, -um
16. savage — saevus, -a, -um
17. small — parvus, -a, -um
18. wicked — malus, -a, -um
19. beautiful — pulcher, -chra, -chrum
20. handsome — pulcher, -chra, -chrum
21. miserable — miser, -era, -erum
22. unhappy — miser, -era, -erum
23. wretched — miser, -era, -erum

Nouns

24. dinner — cena, -ae f.
25. girl — puella, -ae f.
26. letter — epistula, -ae f.
27. maidservant — ancilla, -ae f.
28. meal — cena, -ae f.
29. money — pecunia, -ae f.
30. queen — regina, -ae f.
31. road — via, -ae f.
32. sailor — nauta, -ae m.
33. slavegirl — ancilla, -ae f.
34. spear — hasta, -ae f.
35. street — via, -ae f.
36. villa — villa, -ae f.
37. woman — femina, -ae f.
38. friend — amicus, -i m.
39. god — deus, -i m.
40. horse — equus, -i m.
41. master — dominus, -i m.
42. slave — servus, -i m.
43. son — filius, -i m.
44. sword — gladius, -i m.
45. wall — murus, -i m.
46. book — liber, libri m.
47. boy — puer, -i m.
48. man — vir, viri m.
49. teacher — magister, -tri m.
50. temple — templum, -i n.
51. town — oppidum, -i n.
52. wine — vinum, -i n.

Prepositions

53. (away) from — a/ab + abl.
54. in, on — in + abl.
55. into, onto — in + abl.
56. near — prope + acc.
57. out of — e/ex + abl.
58. to, towards — ad + acc.
59. with — cum + abl.

Verbs

60. build — aedifico, -are, -avi (1)
61. call — voco, -are, -avi (1)
62. carry — porto, -are, -avi (1)
63. enter — intro, -are, -avi (1)
64. fight — pugno, -are, -avi (1)
65. kill — neco, -are, -avi (1)
66. like — amo, -are, -avi (1)
67. look at — specto, -are, -avi (1)
68. love — amo, -are, -avi (1)
69. praise — laudo, -are, -avi (1)
70. prepare — paro, -are, -avi (1)
71. shout — clamo, -are, -avi (1)
72. walk — ambulo, -are, -avi (1)
73. watch — specto, -are, -avi (1)
74. fear — timeo, -ere -ui (2)
75. have — habeo, -ere, -ui (2)
76. destroy — deleo, -ere delevi (2)
77. see — video, -ere, vidi (2)
78. warn — moneo, -ere, -ui (2)
79. be — sum, esse, fui (irreg)

Others

80. always — semper
81. and — et
82. at last — tandem
83. at once — statim
84. finally — tandem
85. however — tamen
86. immediately — statim
87. never — numquam
88. not — non
89. often — saepe
90. soon — mox

Grammar Reference

List 4A: Grammatical terms

adjectives	These are words that describe nouns. e.g. *bonus* (good*), pulcher* (beautiful), *fortis* (brave).
adverbs	These are words which describe how, when or where something happens. e.g. *bene* (well), *statim* (immediately), *hic* (here).
cardinal number	*unus* (one), *duo* (two), *tres* (three) etc.
case	nominative (subject), vocative (person spoken to), accusative (object), genitive (of), dative (to or for) or ablative (by, with, from).
comparative adjective	An adjective comparing something to something else: 'more….' e.g. *fortior* (braver). See also **positive adjective** and **superlative adjective.**
conjugation	A family of verbs which behave in the same way. e.g. *amo* (1) is in the first conjugation; *audio* (4) is in the fourth conjugation.
conjunction	A joining word. e.g. *et* (and), *sed* (but).
declension	A family of nouns which behave in the same way. e.g. *puella* (girl) is in the first declension; *servus* (slave) is in the second declension.
gender	Whether a noun or adjective is masculine, feminine or neuter.
imperative	An order. e.g. *audi!* (listen!), *amate!* (love!).
infinitive	A to-word, the second principal part of a verb, usually ending in *-re* in Latin. e.g. *amare* (to love). But beware of *esse* (to be) and *posse* (to be able)
noun	A person, place or thing.
number	Whether a noun or verb is singular or plural.
person	1st person singular = I; 2nd person singular = You 3rd person singular = He, She, It; 1st person plural = We; 2nd person plural = You; 3rd person plural = They
positive adjective	The usual dictionary form of an adjective, e.g. *bonus, pulcher, fortis, ingens*. See also **comparative adjective** and **superlative adjective**.
prepositions	Little words like *cum* (with), *ad* (to, towards), *in* (in). In Latin, some prepositions are followed by accusative words, others by ablative words.
superlative adjective	An adjective ending in *-issimus* or *-errimus*, meaning 'very' or 'most'. e.g. *fortissimus* (very brave, bravest). See also **positive adjective** and **comparative adjective**.
tense	This describes the time when something is happening. You have met five tenses: present (happening now, e.g. *amo*), imperfect (continuous action in the past, e.g. *amabam*), perfect (a single, one-off action in the past, e.g. *amavi*), future (the will-tense, e.g. *amabo*), pluperfect (the had-tense, e.g. *amaveram*).
verb	A doing word.

List 4b: Nouns

4b.1 Summary of case usage

name of case	job	examples
nominative	subject (doer) of verb	**servus** laborat. *The <u>slave</u> is working.*
	with the verb *to be*	Marcus est **miles.** *Marcus is a <u>soldier</u>.*
vocative	person spoken to	**serve**, quid facis? *<u>Slave</u>, what are you doing?*
accusative	object (receiver) of verb	**servum** punio. *I am punishing the <u>slave</u>.*
	after prepositions like *ad*	ad **servum** currit. *He is running <u>towards the slave</u>.*
genitive	'of'	dominus **servi** est saevus. *The master <u>of the slave</u> is cruel.*
dative	'to', 'for'	pecuniam **servo** dat. *He gives money <u>to the slave</u>.*
ablative	'by', 'with', 'from'	puerum **gladio** vulnerat. *He wounds the boy <u>with his sword</u>.*
	after prepositions like *cum*	cum **servo** pugnat. *He is fighting <u>with the slave</u>.*

4b.2 Summary of Nouns

Declension:	1	2	2	2	2
Gender:	f	m	m	m	n
	girl	slave	boy	field	war
SINGULAR					
nominative	puella	servus	puer	ager	bellum
vocative	puella	serve	puer	ager	bellum
accusative	puellam	servum	puerum	agrum	bellum
genitive	puellae	servi	pueri	agri	belli
dative	puellae	servo	puero	agro	bello
ablative	puella	servo	puero	agro	bello
PLURAL	girls	slaves	boys	fields	wars
nominative	puellae	servi	pueri	agri	bella
vocative	puellae	servi	pueri	agri	bella
accusative	puellas	servos	pueros	agros	bella
genitive	puellarum	servorum	puerorum	agrorum	bellorum
dative	puellis	servis	pueris	agris	bellis
ablative	puellis	servis	pueris	agris	bellis

Declension:	3	3	3
Gender:	m/f	n	n
	king	wound	sea
SINGULAR			
nominative	rex	vulnus	mare
vocative	rex	vulnus	mare
accusative	regem	vulnus	mare
genitive	regis	vulneris	maris
dative	regi	vulneri	mari
ablative	rege	vulnere	mari
PLURAL	kings	wounds	seas
nominative	reges	vulnera	maria
vocative	reges	vulnera	maria
accusative	reges	vulnera	maria
genitive	regum	vulnerum	does not exist!
dative	regibus	vulneribus	maribus
ablative	regibus	vulneribus	maribus

List 4c: Adjectives

4c.1: Adjectives in *-us*

e.g. bon**us**, *good*

	masculine	feminine	neuter
SINGULAR			
nominative	bon**us**	bon**a**	bon**um**
vocative	bon**e**	bon**a**	bon**um**
accusative	bon**um**	bon**am**	bon**um**
genitive	bon**i**	bon**ae**	bon**i**
dative	bon**o**	bon**ae**	bon**o**
ablative	bon**o**	bon**a**	bon**o**
PLURAL			
nominative	bon**i**	bon**ae**	bon**a**
vocative	bon**i**	bon**ae**	bon**a**
accusative	bon**os**	bon**as**	bon**a**
genitive	bon**orum**	bon**arum**	bon**orum**
dative	bon**is**	bon**is**	bon**is**
ablative	bon**is**	bon**is**	bon**is**

4c.2 Adjectives in *-er* (keeping the *e*)

e.g. mis**er**, *miserable*

	masculine	feminine	neuter
SINGULAR			
nominative	miser	miser**a**	miser**um**
vocative	miser	miser**a**	miser**um**
accusative	miser**um**	miser**am**	miser**um**
genitive	miser**i**	miser**ae**	miser**i**
dative	miser**o**	miser**ae**	miser**o**
ablative	miser**o**	miser**a**	miser**o**
PLURAL			
nominative	miser**i**	miser**ae**	miser**a**
vocative	miser**i**	miser**ae**	miser**a**
accusative	miser**os**	miser**as**	miser**a**
genitive	miser**orum**	miser**arum**	miser**orum**
dative	miser**is**	miser**is**	miser**is**
ablative	miser**is**	miser**is**	miser**is**

4c.3 Adjectives in -er (dropping the e)

e.g. pulch**er**, *beautiful*

	masculine	feminine	neuter
SINGULAR			
nominative	pulcher	pulchra	pulchrum
vocative	pulcher	pulchra	pulchrum
accusative	pulchrum	pulchram	pulchrum
genitive	pulchri	pulchrae	pulchri
dative	pulchro	pulchrae	pulchro
ablative	pulchro	pulchra	pulchro
PLURAL			
nominative	pulchri	pulchrae	pulchra
vocative	pulchri	pulchrae	pulchra
accusative	pulchros	pulchras	pulchra
genitive	pulchrorum	pulchrarum	pulchrorum
dative	pulchris	pulchris	pulchris
ablative	pulchris	pulchris	pulchris

4c.4 Third Declension Adjectives in -is

e.g. fort**is** *brave, strong*

	masculine	feminine	neuter
SINGULAR			
nominative	fortis	fortis	forte
vocative	fortis	fortis	forte
accusative	fortem	fortem	forte
genitive	fortis	fortis	fortis
dative	forti	forti	forti
ablative	forti	forti	forti
PLURAL			
nominative	fortes	fortes	fortia
vocative	fortes	fortes	fortia
accusative	fortes	fortes	fortia
genitive	fortium	fortium	fortium
dative	fortibus	fortibus	fortibus
ablative	fortibus	fortibus	fortibus

4c.5 Third Declension Adjectives in -*x*

e.g. audax, *bold*

	masculine	feminine	neuter
SINGULAR			
nominative	auda**x**	auda**x**	auda**x**
vocative	auda**x**	auda**x**	auda**x**
accusative	audac**em**	audac**em**	auda**x**
genitive	audac**is**	audac**is**	audac**is**
dative	audac**i**	audac**i**	audac**i**
ablative	audac**i**	audac**i**	audac**i**
PLURAL			
nominative	audac**es**	audac**es**	audac**ia**
vocative	audac**es**	audac**es**	audac**ia**
accusative	audac**es**	audac**es**	audac**ia**
genitive	audac**ium**	audac**ium**	audac**ium**
dative	audac**ibus**	audac**ibus**	audac**ibus**
ablative	audac**ibus**	audac**ibus**	audac**ibus**

4c.6 Third Declension Adjectives in -*ns*

e.g. inge**ns**, *huge*

	masculine	feminine	neuter
SINGULAR			
nominative	ingens	ingens	ingens
vocative	ingens	ingens	ingens
accusative	ingent**em**	ingent**em**	ingens
genitive	ingent**is**	ingent**is**	ingent**is**
dative	ingent**i**	ingent**i**	ingent**i**
ablative	ingent**i**	ingent**i**	ingent**i**
PLURAL			
nominative	ingent**es**	ingent**es**	ingent**ia**
vocative	ingent**es**	ingent**es**	ingent**ia**
accusative	ingent**es**	ingent**es**	ingent**ia**
genitive	ingent**ium**	ingent**ium**	ingent**ium**
dative	ingent**ibus**	ingent**ibus**	ingent**ibus**
ablative	ingent**ibus**	ingent**ibus**	ingent**ibus**

4c.7 Comparison

Here are some examples:

	Positive	Comparative	Superlative
-us		**stem + ior**	**stem + issimus**
	altus *high*	altior *higher*	altissimus *highest/very high*
-er		**stem + ior**	**positive + rimus**
	miser *miserable* pulcher *beautiful*	miserior *more miserable* pulchrior *more beautiful*	miserrimus *very miserable* pulcherrimus *very beautiful*
-is **-x** **-ns**		**stem + ior**	**stem + issimus**
	fortis *brave* audax *daring* ingens *huge*	fortior *more brave* audacior *more daring* ingentior *more huge*	fortissimus *very brave, the bravest* audacissimus *very daring* ingentissimus *very huge*

4c.8 Comparative adjectives in *-ior*

e.g. fort**ior**, *braver*

	masculine	feminine	neuter
SINGULAR			
nominative	fort**ior**	fort**ior**	fort**ius**
vocative	fort**ior**	fort**ior**	fort**ius**
accusative	forti**orem**	fortior**em**	fort**ius**
genitive	fortior**is**	fortior**is**	fortior**is**
dative	fortior**i**	fortior**i**	fortior**i**
ablative	fortior**e**	fortior**e**	fortior**e**
PLURAL			
nominative	fortior**es**	fortior**es**	fortior**a**
vocative	fortior**es**	fortior**es**	fortior**a**
accusative	fortior**es**	fortior**es**	fortior**a**
genitive	fortior**um**	fortior**um**	fortior**um**
dative	fortior**ibus**	fortior**ibus**	fortior**ibus**
ablative	fortior**ibus**	fortior**ibus**	fortior**ibus**

4c.9 Irregular Comparison of Adjectives

Positive	Comparative	Superlative
bonus, *good*	melior, *better*	optimus, *very good, best*
malus, *bad*	peior, *worse*	pessimus, *very bad, worst*
magnus, *big*	maior, *bigger*	maximus, *very big, biggest*
parvus, *small*	minor, *smaller*	minimus, *very small, smallest*
multus, *much, many*	plus, *more*	plurimus, *most, very many*

4c.10 *plus, pluris*

singular (noun)		
nominative	plus	
vocative	plus	
accusative	plus	
genitive	pluris	
dative	(does not exist)	
ablative	plure	

plural (adjective)	masculine	feminine	neuter
nominative	plures	plures	plura
vocative	plures	plures	plura
accusative	plures	plures	plura
genitive	plurium	plurium	plurium
dative	pluribus	pluribus	pluribus
ablative	pluribus	pluribus	pluribus

List 5: Pronouns

5.1 First Person Pronoun: *ego*

	singular		plural	
nominative	ego	*I*	nos	*we*
accusative	me	*me*	nos	*us*
genitive	mei	*of me/my*	nostrum	*of us/our*
dative	mihi	*to/for me*	nobis	*to/for us*
ablative	me	*(by) me*	nobis	*(by) us*
note:	mecum	*with me*	nobiscum	*with us*

5.2 Second Person Pronoun: *tu*

	singular		plural	
nominative	tu	*you*	vos	*you*
accusative	te	*you*	vos	*you*
genitive	tui	*of you/your*	vestrum	*of you/your*
dative	tibi	*to/for you*	vobis	*to/for you*
ablative	te	*(by) you*	vobis	*(by) you*
note:	tecum	*with you*	vobiscum	*with you*

5.3 Third person pronoun: *is, ea, id* (= *he, she, it; that, those*)

singular	masculine		feminine		neuter	
nominative	is	*he*	ea	*she*	id	*it*
accusative	eum	*him*	eam	*her*	id	*it*
genitive	eius	*his (of him)*	eius	*her (of her)*	eius	*of it*
dative	ei	*to/for him*	ei	*to/for her*	ei	*to/for it*
ablative	eo	*by him*	ea	*by her*	eo	*by it*
plural						
nominative	ei	*they*	eae	*they*	ea	*they*
accusative	eos	*them*	eas	*them*	ea	*them*
genitive	eorum	*their (of them)*	earum	*their (of them)*	eorum	*their (of them)*
dative	eis	*to/for them*	eis	*to/for them*	eis	*to/for them*
ablative	eis	*by them*	eis	*by them*	eis	*by them*

5.4 Third person reflexive pronoun

	singular		plural	
nominative		*(cannot exist)*		*(cannot exist)*
accusative	se	*himself/herself*	se	*themselves*
genitive	sui	*of himself/of herself*	sui	*of themselves*
dative	sibi	*to/for himself/herself*	sibi	*to/for themselves*
ablative	se	*(by) himself/herself*	se	*(by) themselves*
note:	secum	*with him/with her*	secum	*with them*

5.5 Summary of reflexive pronouns

	singular		plural	
1st person	me	*myself*	nos	*ourselves*
2nd person	te	*yourself*	vos	*yourselves*
3rd person	se	*himself/herself/itself*	se	*themselves*

List 6: Prepositions

6.1 Level 1

ad + accusative	*to, towards*	ad reginam ambulat. *He is walking towards the queen.*
contra + accusative	*against*	contra nautam pugnat. *He is fighting against the sailor.*
per + accusative	*through, along*	per viam currit. *He is running along the road.*
prope + accusative	*near*	prope murum stat. *He is standing near the wall.*
trans + accusative	*across*	trans viam festinat. *He hurries across the road.*
a/ab + ablative	(*away*) *from*	ab insula navigat. *He sails away from the island.*
cum + ablative	*with*	cum amico ludit. *He is playing with a friend.*
de + ablative	*down from, about*	de periculo monet. *He warns about the danger.*
e/ex + ablative	*out of*	ex oppido currit. *He runs out of the town.*

The Preposition *in*
This frequently causes problems, because it can be followed by an ablative word (when it means *in* or *on*.) as well as by an accusative word (when it means *into*).

Examples
in + ablative = *in*.   equus in ag**ro** currit.
                          *The horse is running **in** the field.*

in + accusative = *into*.   equus in ag**rum** currit.
                              *The horse is running **into** the field.*

6.2 Level 2

ante + accusative	*before*	ante proelium timet. *He is afraid before the battle.*
circum + accusative	*around*	circum insulam navigat. *He sails around the island.*
inter + accusative	*among, between*	inter equos currit. *He runs between the horses.*
post + accusative	*after, behind*	post patrem ambulat. *He is walking behind his father.*
pro + ablative	*on behalf of, for, in front of*	pro domino pugnat. *He fights for his master.*
propter + accusative	*because of*	propter periculum fugit. *He flees because of the danger.*
super + accusative	*above*	super aquam stat. *He is standing above the water.*
sine + ablative	*without*	sine gladio pugnat. *He is fighting without a sword.*
sub + ablative	*under*	sub equo dormit. *He is sleeping under the horse.*

List 7: Verbs

7.1 Present Tense

	1 *love*	2 *warn*	3 *rule*	3½ *take*	4 *hear*
I	am**o**	mon**eo**	reg**o**	cap**io**	aud**io**
You (sg)	am**as**	mon**es**	reg**is**	cap**is**	aud**is**
He/She/It	am**at**	mon**et**	reg**it**	cap**it**	aud**it**
We	am**amus**	mon**emus**	reg**imus**	cap**imus**	aud**imus**
You (pl)	am**atis**	mon**etis**	reg**itis**	cap**itis**	aud**itis**
They	am**ant**	mon**ent**	reg**unt**	cap**iunt**	aud**iunt**

7.2 Imperfect Tense

	1 *was/were loving*	2 *was/were warning*	3 *was/were ruling*	3½ *was/were taking*	4 *was/were hearing*
I	am**abam**	mon**ebam**	reg**ebam**	cap**iebam**	aud**iebam**
You (sg)	am**abas**	mon**ebas**	reg**ebas**	cap**iebas**	aud**iebas**
He/She/It	am**abat**	mon**ebat**	reg**ebat**	cap**iebat**	aud**iebat**
We	am**abamus**	mon**ebamus**	reg**ebamus**	cap**iebamus**	aud**iebamus**
You (pl)	am**abatis**	mon**ebatis**	reg**ebatis**	cap**iebatis**	aud**iebatis**
They	am**abant**	mon**ebant**	reg**ebant**	cap**iebant**	aud**iebant**

7.3 Perfect Tense

	1 *loved*	2 *warned*	3 *ruled*	3½ *took*	4 *heard*
I	ama**vi**	mon**ui**	rex**i**	cep**i**	audi**vi**
You (sg)	ama**visti**	mon**uisti**	rex**isti**	cep**isti**	audi**visti**
He/She/It	ama**vit**	mon**uit**	rex**it**	cep**it**	audi**vit**
We	ama**vimus**	mon**uimus**	rex**imus**	cep**imus**	audi**vimus**
You (pl)	ama**vistis**	mon**uistis**	rex**istis**	cep**istis**	audi**vistis**
They	ama**verunt**	mon**uerunt**	rex**erunt**	cep**erunt**	audi**verunt**

7.4 Present Infinitives

	Present	English	Infinitive	English
1	amo	*I love*	am**are**	*to love*
2	moneo	*I warn*	mon**ere**	*to warn*
3	rego	*I rule*	reg**ere**	*to rule*
3½	capio	*I take*	cap**ere**	*to take*
4	audio	*I hear*	aud**ire**	*to hear*
irregular verb	sum	*I am*	esse	*to be*

7.5 Imperatives

	singular	plural	
1	am**a**	am**ate**	*love!*
2	mon**e**	mon**ete**	*warn!*
3	reg**e**	reg**ite**	*rule!*
4	aud**i**	aud**ite**	*hear!/listen!*
3½	cap**e**	cap**ite**	*take*

7.6 Future Tense

	1 *will love*	2 *will warn*	3 *will rule*	3½ *will take*	4 *will hear*
I	ama**bo**	mone**bo**	reg**am**	capi**am**	audi**am**
You (sg)	ama**bis**	mone**bis**	reg**es**	capi**es**	audi**es**
He/She/It	ama**bit**	mone**bit**	reg**et**	capi**et**	audi**et**
We	ama**bimus**	mone**bimus**	reg**emus**	capi**emus**	audi**emus**
You (pl)	ama**bitis**	mone**bitis**	reg**etis**	capi**etis**	audi**etis**
They	ama**bunt**	mone**bunt**	reg**ent**	capi**ent**	audi**ent**

7.7 Pluperfect Tense

	1 *had loved*	2 *had warned*	3 *had ruled*	3½ *had taken*	4 *had heard*
I	amav**eram**	monu**eram**	rex**eram**	cep**eram**	audiv**eram**
You (sg)	amav**eras**	monu**eras**	rex**eras**	cep**eras**	audiv**eras**
He/She/It	amav**erat**	monu**erat**	rex**erat**	cep**erat**	audiv**erat**
We	amav**eramus**	monu**eramus**	rex**eramus**	cep**eramus**	audiv**eramus**
You (pl)	amav**eratis**	monu**eratis**	rex**eratis**	cep**eratis**	audiv**eratis**
They	amav**erant**	monu**erant**	rex**erant**	cep**erant**	audiv**erant**

7.8 *sum, I am*

	Present *am/is/are*	Imperfect *was/were*	Perfect *was/were*	Future *will be*	Pluperfect *had been*
I	sum	eram	fui	ero	fueram
You (sg)	es	eras	fuisti	eris	fueras
He/She/It	est	erat	fuit	erit	fuerat
We	sumus	eramus	fuimus	erimus	fueramus
You (pl	estis	eratis	fuistis	eritis	fueratis
They	sunt	erant	fuerunt	erunt	fuerant

Infinitive ('to')	esse
Imperatives	
singular:	es/esto
plural:	este/estote

103

7.4 *possum*, I am able, can

	Present *can*	**Imperfect** *could*	**Perfect** *could*	**Future** *will be able*	**Pluperfect** *had been able*
I	possum	poteram	potui	potero	potueram
You (sg)	potes	poteras	potuisti	poteris	potueras
He/She/It	potest	poterat	potuit	poterit	potuerat
We	possumus	poteramus	potuimus	poterimus	potueramus
You (pl)	potestis	poteratis	potuistis	poteritis	potueratis
They	possunt	poterant	potuerunt	poterunt	potuerant
Infinitive (*to*)	posse				

List 8: Syntax

8.1 Adverbs

Adverbs do not change their form in Latin. They will usually be found just before the verb at the end of the sentence.

servi <u>fortiter</u> pugnant.   *The slaves fight bravely.*
pueri <u>semper</u> <u>bene</u> laborant.   *Boys always work well.*

8.2 *quod* (= because) clauses
These are straightforward:

puella nautam amabat <u>quod</u> pecuniam habebat.
The girl liked the sailor <u>because</u> he had money.

servi, <u>quod</u> dominum timebant, fugerunt.
<u>Because</u> the slaves were afraid of their master, they fled.

8.3 ubi (= when) **clauses**
These also are straighforward:

<u>ubi</u> magistrum vidit, timuit.
<u>When</u> he saw the enemy, he was afraid.

servi, <u>ubi</u> pericula viderunt, cucurrerunt.
<u>When</u> the slaves saw the dangers, they ran.

8.4 Direct Questions: -ne

A Latin statement can be changed into a question be adding *–ne* to the end of the <u>first word</u> of the sentence and adding a question mark to the end of the sentence:

<u>Examples</u>

1.   laborat.   *He is working.*
         laborat**ne?**   *Is he working?*

2.   est fessus.   *He is tired.*
         est**ne** fessus?   *Is he tired?*

3.   puer puellam spectat.   *The boy is looking at the girl.*
         puer**ne** puellam spectat?   *Is the boy looking at the girl?*

8.5 Present infinitives

You will find present infinitives used with the verbs *prepare* (**paro**), *want* (**cupio**), *decide* (**constituo**) and *order* (**iubeo**). The infinitive usually comes just before the main verb at the end of the sentence.

puella **cantare** parat.   *The girl prepares **to sing**.*
pueri **ludere** cupiunt.   *The boys want **to play**.*
servi **pugnare** constituerunt.   *The slaves decided **to fight**.*
dominus servos bene **laborare** iussit.   *The master ordered the slaves **to work** well.*

8.6 quamquam (*=although*) **clauses**
These are straightforward:

<u>quamquam</u> femina pecuniam habebat, virum non habebat.
<u>Although</u> the woman had money, she did not have a husband.

milites, <u>quamquam</u> fessi erant, bene pugnaverunt.
<u>Although</u> the soldiers were tired, they fought well.

8.7 Comparisons with quam (*=than*)
quam (*than*) is used to compare things. The nouns being compared are always in the same case.

Iulius Caesar miles clarior **quam** Alexander Magnus erat.
*Julius Caesar was a more famous soldier **than** Alexander the Great.*

puellae sapientiores **quam** pueri sunt.
*Girls are wiser **than** boys.*

8.8 Direct Questions: *nonne* and *num*

nonne can be added to the start of a sentence to indicate that the answer 'yes' is expected. How you actually translate this word will depend on the sentence.

<u>Example</u>   nonne laborat?   *He is working, isn't he?*
    Surely he is working?

num can be added to the start of a sentence to indicate that the answer 'no' is expected. How you actually translate this word will depend on the sentence.

<u>Example</u>   num laborat?   *He is not working, is he?*
    Surely he is not working?

8.9 Prohibitions

Prohibitions are commands telling someone NOT to do something. In English they begin with the words *Do not....*

In Latin singular prohibitions (telling one person not to do something) begin with the word **noli**.

Plural prohibitions (telling more than one person not to do something) begin with the word **nolite**.

The **noli/nolite** is followed by a present infinitive.

noli currere, puer!   *Do not run, boy!*   (singular prohibition)
nolite currere, pueri!   *Do not run, boys!*   (plural prohibition)

8.10 Reflexive Pronouns

These are pronouns which reflect ('bend back') the action to the subject. The subject of the verb is also its object.

me cras necabo.
*I shall kill **myself** tomorrow.*

is puer **se** amat.
*That boy likes **himself**.*

cur **vos** non defenditis, milites?
*Why are you not defending **yourselves**, soldiers?*

cives **se** hostibus tradiderunt.
*The citizens handed **themselves** over to the enemy.*

List 9: Cardinal numbers

unus	one
duo	two
tres	three
quattuor	four
quinque	five
sex	six
septem	seven
octo	eight
novem	nine
decem	ten
undecim	eleven
duodecim	twelve
tredecim	thirteen
quattuordecim	fourteen
quindecim	fifteen
sedecim	sixteen
septendecim	seventeen
duodeviginti	eighteen
undeviginti	nineteen
viginti	twenty

Latin CE Level 1 Revision Check-list

	topic	quick reminder	example	1st check			2nd check		
				☹	😐	☺	☹	😐	☺
nouns	1st declension	mostly f.	puella						
	2nd declension	m.	servus						
	2nd declension	m. (keeping the *e*)	puer						
	2nd declension	m. (dropping the *e*)	ager						
	2nd declension	n.	bellum						
verbs	present tense	is/are 1st conjugation	amo						
		2nd conjugation	moneo						
		3rd conjugation	rego						
		4th conjugation	audio						
		to be - irreg	sum						
verbs	imperfect tense	was/were –ing, used to… 1st	amabam						
		2nd conjugation	monebam						
		3rd conjugation	regebam						
		4th conjugation	audiebam						
		to be - irreg	eram						
verbs	perfect tense	single action in past 1st	amavi						
		2nd conjugation	monui						
		3rd conjugation	rexi						
		4th conjugation	audivi						
		to be - irreg	fui						
verbs	infinitives	*to*-words 1st	amare						
		2nd conjugation	monere						
		3rd conjugation	regere						
		4th conjugation	audire						
		to be - irreg	esse						
verbs	imperatives	commands 1st	ama, amate						
		2nd conjugation	mone, monete						
		3rd conjugation	rege, regite						
		4th conjugation	audi, audite						
		to be - irreg	es/esto, este/estote						
adjectives	-us	servus/puella/bellum endings	bonus						
	-er	keeping the *e*	miser						
	-er	dropping the *e*	pulcher						
pronouns	*I* and *you*	*ego* and *tu*	ego/nos, tu/vos						
numbers		1-10	unus - decem						
GRAMMAR	cases	*what do they mean?*	nominative						
			vocative						
			accusative						
			genitive						
			dative						
			ablative						
	persons	I/we	1st						
		you	2nd						
		he/she/it/they	3rd						
	number	singular							
		plural							
	questions	(on end of first word)	-ne ?						
+ vocabulary!									

Latin CE Level 2 Revision Check-list

Level 1 list +:

	topic	quick reminder	example	1st check			2nd check		
				☹	😐	☺	☹	😐	☺
nouns	3rd decl m/f		rex, regis						
	3rd decl n		vulnus, vulneris						
verbs	future 1st/2nd	'will' tense	-bo, -bis, -bit						
	future 3rd/4th	'will' tense	-am, -es, -et						
	future, *to be*		ero, eris, erit						
	pluperfect	'had' tense	amaveram						
	possum	I am able	possum						
adjectives	3rd decl	in -is	fortis						
		in -x	audax						
		in -ns	ingens						
		in -ior	fortior, *braver*						
	comparison	-ior + quam	fortior, *braver*						
	irregular comparison		bonus						
			malus						
			magnus						
			parvus						
			multus						
pronouns	he, she, it	is, ea, id							
	I	ego							
	You	tu							
	reflexives	se							
questions	nonne	expecting a yes	nonne pugnas?						
	num	expecting a no	num pugnas?						
prohibitions	noli/nolite + infinitive	do not...!	noli currere!						
numbers	11-20								
+ vocabulary!									

List 10: English-Latin Quick Reference

sg. = singular   pl. = plural   abl. = ablative   acc. = accusative   infin. = infinitive   irreg. = irregular

able, be	possum, posse, potui (irreg.)	because	quod
about	de + abl.	because of	propter + acc.
above	super + abl.	before	ante + acc.; antequam
across	trans + acc.	between	inter + acc.
after	post + acc.; postquam	be wrong	erro, -are (1)
afterwards	postea	big	magnus, -a, -um
again	iterum	body	corpus, corporis n.
against	contra + acc.	bold	audax, audacis
alive	vivus, -a, -um	book	liber, libri m.
all	omnis, -is, -e	both … and …	et … et …
ally	socius, -i m.	boy	puer, pueri m.
alone	solus, -a, -um	brave	fortis, -is, -e
along	per + acc.	bravely	fortiter
already	iam	bravery	virtus, virtutis f.
also	etiam; quoque	bright	clarus, -a, -um
although	quamquam	brother	frater, fratris m.
always	semper	build	aedifico, -are (1)
am	sum, esse, fui (irreg.)	but	sed
am away	absum, abesse, afui (irreg.)	by chance	forte
among	inter + acc.	call	voco, -are (1)
am present	adsum, adesse, adfui (irreg.)	can (= be able)	possum, posse, potui (irreg.)
and	et; -que	capture	capio, -ere, cepi (3½)
and so	itaque	carry	porto, -are (1)
anger	ira, -ae f.	carry on	gero, -ere, gessi (3)
angry	iratus, -a, -um	catch sight of	conspicio, -ere, conspexi (3½)
announce	nuntio, -are (1)	chance, by	forte
answer	respondeo, -ere, respondi (2)	charge	ruo, -ere, rui (3)
		children	liberi, liberorum m. pl.
approach	appropinquo, -are, appropinquavi (1)	choose	lego, -ere, legi (3)
		citizen	civis, -is m.
arms (= weapons)	arma, -orum n. pl.	city	urbs, urbis f.
around	circum + acc.	clear	clarus, -a, -um
arrive	advenio, -ire, adveni (4)	collect	colligo, -ere, collegi (3)
arrow	sagitta, -ae f.	come	venio, -ire, veni (4)
ask, ask for	rogo, -are (1)	companion	comes, comitis m.
at last	tandem	comrade	socius, -i m.
attack	oppugno, -are (1)	conquer	vinco, -ere, vici (3); supero, -are (1)
away from	a/ab + abl.	could (= was able)	possum, posse, potui (irreg.)
bad	malus, -a, -um	country	patria, -ae f.
battle	proelium, -i n.	courage	virtus, virtutis f.
be	sum, esse, fui (irreg.)	crowd	turba, -ae f.
beat	supero, -are (1); vinco, -ere, vici (3)	cruel	crudelis, -is, -e
beautiful	pulcher, -chra, -chrum		

danger	periculum, -i n.
daring	audax, audacis
daughter	filia, -ae f.
dead	mortuus, -a, -um
dear	carus, -a, -um
death	mors, mortis f.
decide	constituo, -ere, constitui (3)
deep	altus, -a, -um
defend	defendo, -ere, defendi (3)
delay	mora, -ae f.
depart	discedo, -ere, -cessi (3)
destroy	deleo, -ere, delevi (2)
difficult	difficilis, -is, -e
dinner	cena, -ae f.
do	facio, -ere, feci (3½)
do not …!	noli (sg.) / nolite (pl.) + infin.
down from	de + abl.
drink	bibo, -ere, bibi (3)
easy	facilis, -is, -e
eat	consumo, -ere, -sumpsi (3)
eight	octo
eighteen	duodeviginti
eleven	undecim
enemy	hostes, hostium m. pl.
enter	intro, -are (1)
escape	effugio, -ere, effugi (3½)
especially	magnopere
even	etiam
every	omnis, -is, -e
everyone	omnes (m. pl.)
everything	omnia (n. pl.)
evil	malus, -a, -um
ex-slave	libertus, -i m.
famous	clarus, -a, -um
farmer	agricola, -ae m.
father	pater, patris m.
fear	timeo, -ere, timui (2)
few	pauci, -ae, -a (pl.)
field	ager, agri m.
fifteen	quindecim
fight	pugno, -are (1)
finally	tandem
find	invenio, -ire, inveni (4)
five	quinque
flee	fugio, -ere, fugi (3½)
food	cibus, -i m.
for	nam
for (= on behalf of)	pro + abl.
for a long time	diu
forces	copiae, -arum f. pl.
forest	silva, -ae f.

form a plan	consilium capio, -ere, cepi (3½)
fourteen	quattuordecim
fortunate	felix, felicis
forum	forum, -i n.
four	quattuor
free (= set free)	libero, -are (1)
freedman	libertus, -i m.
friend	amicus, -i m.
frighten	terreo, -ere, terrui (2)
from	a/ab + abl.
garden	hortus, -i m.
general	dux, ducis m.
girl	puella, -ae f.
gift	donum, -i n.
give	do, dare, dedi (1)
god	deus, -i m.
goddess	dea, -ae f.
go in	intro, -are(1)
gold	aurum, -i n.
good	bonus, -a, -um
great	magnus, -a, -um
greatly	magnopere
Greece	Graecia, -ae f.
Greek	Graecus, -a, -um
greet	saluto, -are (1)
ground	terra, -ae f.
hand over	trado, -ere, tradidi (3)
handsome	pulcher, -chra, -chrum
happy	laetus, -a, -um
have	habeo, -ere, habui (2)
have to	debeo, -ere, debui (2) + infin.
hear	audio, -ire, audivi (4)
help	auxilium, -i n.
her (own)	suus, -a, -um
here	hic
herself	se
high	altus, -a, -um
himself	se
his (own)	suus, -a, -um
hold	teneo, -ere, tenui (2)
holy	sacer, sacra, sacrum
homeland	patria, -ae f.
horse	equus, -i m.
house	villa, -ae f.
however	tamen; autem
huge	ingens, ingentis
hurry	festino, -are (1)
husband	maritus, -i m.

I	ego	move	moveo, -ere, movi (2)
immediately	statim	much	multus, -a, -um
in	in + abl.	must	debeo, -ere, debui (2) + infin.
inhabitant	incola, -ae m.	my	meus, -a, -um
in this way	sic		
into	in + acc.	name	nomen, nominis n.
in vain	frustra	near	prope + acc.
island	insula, -ae f.	never	numquam
		next	deinde
journey	iter, itineris n.	nine	novem
		nineteen	undeviginti
kill	neco, -are (1);	noble	nobilis, -is, -e
	occido, -ere, occidi (3)	noone	nemo
king	rex, regis m.	not	non
		nothing	nihil
land	terra, -ae f.	now	iam; nunc
laugh	rideo, ere, risi (2)		
lead	duco, -ere, duxi (3)	often	saepe
lead back	reduco, -ere, reduxi (3)	old man	senex, senis m.
leader	dux, ducis m.	on	in + abl.
letter	epistula, -ae f.	on account of	propter + acc.
light	lux, lucis f.	one	unus
like	amo, -are (1)	one day	olim
listen/listen to	audio, -ire, audivi (4)	onto	in + acc.
little	parvus, -a, -um	order	iubeo, -ere, iussi (2)
live	habito, -are (1)	our	noster, -tra, -trum
long	longus, -a, -um	out of	e/ex + abl.
look at	specto, -are (1)	overcome	supero, -are (1);
love	amo, -are (1)		vinco, -ere, vici (3)
lucky	felix, felicis		
		parent	parens, parentis m./f.
maidservant	ancilla, -ae f.	part	pars, partis f.
make	facio, -ere, feci (3½)	person	homo, hominis m.
make a mistake	erro, -are (1)	place	locus, -i m.
man	vir, viri m.; homo, hominis m.	plan	consilium, -n.
many	multus, -a, -um	play	ludo, -ere, lusi (3)
march (noun)	iter, itineris n.	poet	poeta, -ae m.
march (verb)	iter facio, -ere, feci (3½)	praise	laudo, -are (1)
market place	forum, -i n.	prepare	paro, -are (1)
master	dominus, -i m.	present	donum, -i n.
meal	cena, -ae f.	present, be	adsum, adesse, adfui
messenger	nuntius, -i m.		(irreg)
middle of	medius, -a, -um	prisoner	captivus, -i m.
mine	meus, -a, -um	punish	punio, -ire, punivi (4)
miserable	miser, misera, miserum	put	pono, -ere, posui (3)
mistake, make a	erro, -are (1)		
mistress	domina, -ae f.	queen	regina, -ae f.
money	pecunia, -ae f.	(question)	-ne
mother	mater, matris f.	quickly	celeriter
mountain	mons, montis m.		

read	lego, -ere, legi (3)	strong	validus, -a, -um
receive	accipio, -ere, accepi (3½)	suddenly	subito
remain	maneo, -ere, mansi (2)	surely?	nonne?
reply	respondeo, -ere, respondi (2)	surely … not?	num?
rest of, the	ceteri, -ae, -a (pl.)	sword	gladius, -i m.
river	flumen, fluminis n.	take	capio, -ere, cepi (3½)
road	via, -ae f.	teacher	magister, -tri m.
Roman	Romanus, -a, -um	tell	narro, -are (1)
Rome	Roma, -ae f.	temple	templum, -i n.
rule	rego, -ere, regi (3)	ten	decem
run	curro, -ere, cucurri (3)	than	quam
run away	fugio, -ere, fugi (3½)	that	(use table of *is, ea, id*)
		their (own)	suus, -a, -um
sacred	sacer, sacra, sacrum	themselves	se
sad	tristis, -is, -e	then	deinde; tum
safe	tutus, -a, -um	there	ibi
said, he/she	inquit	therefore	igitur; itaque
said, they	inquiunt	thirteen	tredecim
sail	navigo, -are (1)	three	tres
sailor	nauta, -ae m.	through	per + acc.
savage	saevus, -a, -um	throw	iacio, -ere, ieci (3½)
save	servo, -are (1)	thus	sic
say	dico, -ere, dixi (3)	tired	fessus, -a, -um
says, he/she	inquit	to	ad + acc.
say, they	inquiunt	today	hodie
sea	mare, maris n.	tomorrow	cras
see	video, -ere, vidi (2)	towards	ad + acc.
seize	occupo, -are (1)	town	oppidum, -i n.
send	mitto, -ere, misi (3)	travel	iter facio, -ere, feci (3½)
set free	libero, -are (1)	Trojan	Troianus, -a, -um
seven	septem	troops	copiae, -arum f. pl.
seventeen	septendecim	Troy	Troia, -ae f.
shield	scutum, -i n.	twelve	duodecim
ship	navis, -is f.	twenty	viginti
shout (noun)	clamor, clamoris m.	two	duo
shout (verb)	clamo, -are (1)		
show	ostendo, -ere, ostendi (3)	under	sub + abl.
sing	canto, -are (1)	unhappy	miser, misera, miserum
sister	soror, sororis f.		
six	sex	vain, in	frustra
sixteen	sedecim	villa	villa, -ae f.
sky	caelum, -i n.	voice	vox, vocis f.
slave	servus, -i m.		
slavegirl	ancilla, -ae f.	wage (a war)	gero, -ere, gessi (3)
sleep	dormio, -ire, -ivi (4)	wait for	exspecto, -are (1)
small	parvus, -a, -um	walk	ambulo, -are (1)
soldier	miles, militis m.	wall	murus, -i m.
son	filius, -i m.	wander	erro, -are (1)
soon	mox	want	cupio, -ere, cupivi (3½)
spear	hasta, -ae f.	war	bellum, -i n.
stand	sto, stare, steti (1)	warn	moneo, -ere, monui (2)
stay	maneo, -ere, mansi (2)	watch	specto, -are (1)
street	via, -ae f.	water	aqua, -ae f.

wave	unda, -ae f.	wood	silva, -ae f.
way	via, -ae f.	woman	femina, -ae f.;
weapons	arma, -orum n. pl.		mulier, mulieris f.
we	nos	word	verbum, -i n.
well	bene	work	laboro, -are (1)
well known	notus, -a, -um	wound (noun)	vulnus, vulneris n.
what?	quid?	wound (verb)	vulnero, -are (1)
when	ubi	wretched	miser, misera, miserum
where?	ubi?	write	scribo, -ere, scripsi (3)
who?	quis?	wrong, be	erro, -are (1)
why?	cur?		
wicked	malus, -a, -um	yesterday	heri
wife	uxor, uxoris f.	you (sg.)	tu
wind	ventus, -i m.	you (pl.)	vos
wine	vinum, -i n.	young man	iuvenis, -is m.
wise	sapiens, sapientis	your (sg.)	tuus, -a, -um
with	cum + abl.	your (pl.)	vester , -tra, -trum
without	sine + abl.		

List 11: Latin-English Quick Reference

sg. = singular   pl. = plural   abl. = ablative   acc. = accusative   infin. = infinitive   irreg. = irregular   perf. = perfect   imperf. = imperfect

a/ab + abl.	away from
abera-	(imperf. of *absum*)
adera-	(imperf. of *adsum*)
adfu-	(perf. of *adsum*)
absum, abesse, afui (irreg.) I am away	
accep-	(perf. of *accipio*)
accipio, -ere, accepi (3½)	I receive
ad + acc.	to, towards
adsum, adesse, adfui (irreg.) I am present	
aedifico (1)	I build
afu-	(perf. of *absum*)
ager, agri m.	field
agricola, -ae m.	farmer
altus, -a, -um	high, deep
ambulo (1)	I walk
amicus, -i m.	friend
amo (1)	I like, love
ancilla, -ae f.	maidservant
aqua, -ae f.	water
audax, audacis	bold, daring
audio, -ire, -ivi (4)	I hear, listen to
aurum, -i n.	gold
auxilium, -i n.	help
bellum, -i n.	war
bene	well
bibo, -ere, bibi (3)	I drink
bonus, -a, -um	good
caelum, -i n.	sky
canto (1)	I sing
capio, -ere, cepi (3½)	I take, capture
captivus, -i m.	prisoner
cena, -ae f.	dinner, meal
cep-	(perf. of *capio*)
cibus, -i m.	food
clamo (1)	I shout
clarus, -a, -um	famous, bright, clear
consilium, -i n.	plan
constituo, -ere, constitui (3) I decide	
consumo, -ere, -sumpsi (3) I eat	
contra + acc.	against
cucurr-	(perf. of *curro*)
cum + abl.	with
cupio, -ere, cupivi (3½)	I want
cur?	why?
curro, -ere, cucurri (3)	I run

de + abl.	down from, about
dea, -ae f.	goddess
decem	ten
ded-	(perf. of *do*)
deinde	then, next
deleo, -ere, delevi (2)	I destroy
deus, -i m.	god
dico, -ere, dixi (3)	I say
discedo, -ere, -cessi (3)	I depart
diu	for a long time
dix-	(perf. of *dico*)
do, dare, dedi (1)	I give
domina, -ae f.	mistress
dominus, -i m.	master
dormio, -ire, dormivi (4)	I sleep
duco, -ere, duxi (3)	I lead
duo	two
dux-	(perf. of *duco*)
e/ex + abl.	out of
ego	I
epistula, -ae f.	letter
equus, -i m.	horse
era-	(imperf. of *sum*)
et	and
etiam	also, even
facio, -ere, feci (3½)	I do, make
fec-	(perf. of *facio*)
femina, -ae f.	woman
fessus, -a, -um	tired
festino (1)	I hurry
filia, -ae f.	daughter
filius, -i m.	son
fortiter	bravely
forum, -i n.	forum, market place
fu-	(perf. of *sum*)
gladius, -i m.	sword
Graecia, -ae f.	Greece
Graecus, -a, -um	Greek
habeo, -ere, habui (2)	I have
habito (1)	I live
hasta, -ae f.	spear
hic	here
hortus, -i m.	garden

iacio, -ere, ieci (3½)	I throw	nuntius, -i m.	messenger
iam	now, already		
ibi	there	octo	eight
iec-	(perf. of *iacio*)	olim	one day
igitur	therefore	oppidum, -i n.	town
in + abl.	in, on	oppugno (1)	I attack
in + acc.	into, onto	ostendo, -ere, ostendi (3)	I show
incola, -ae m.	inhabitant	paro (1)	I prepare
insula, -ae f.	island	parvus, -a, -um	small, little
intro (1)	I enter, go in	patria, -ae f.	homeland, country
ira, -ae f.	anger	pecunia, -ae f.	money
iratus, -a, -um	angry	per + acc.	through, along
itaque	and so, therefore	periculum, -i n.	danger
iterum	again	poeta, -ae m.	poet
iubeo, -ere, iussi (2)	I order	pono, -ere, posui (3)	I put
iuss-	(perf. of *iubeo*)	porto (1)	I carry
		posu-	(perf. of *pono*)
laboro (1)	I work	proelium, -i n.	battle
laetus, -a, -um	happy	prope + acc.	near
laudo (1)	I praise	puella, -ae f.	girl
lego, -ere, legi (3)	I read, choose	puer, pueri m.	boy
liber, libri m.	book	pugno (1)	I fight
libertus, -i m.	freedman, ex-slave	pulcher, -chra, -chrum	beautiful, handsome
locus -i m.	place		
ludo, -ere, lusi (3)	I play	quattuor	four
lus-	(perf. of *ludo*)	quid?	what?
		quinque	five
magister, -tri m.	teacher	quis?	who?
magnopere	greatly, especially	quod	because
magnus, -a, -um	big, great		
malus, -a, -um	bad, evil, wicked	regina, -ae f.	queen
maneo, -ere mansi (2)	I stay, remain	rego, -ere, rexi (3)	I rule
mans-	(perf. of *maneo*)	respondeo, -ere, respondi (2)	I answer, reply
maritus, -i m.	husband	rex-	(perf. of *rego*)
meus, -a, -um	my, mine	rideo, -ere, risi (2)	I laugh
mis-	(perf. of *mitto*)	ris-	(perf. of *rideo*)
miser, misera, miserum	wretched, unhappy	rogo (1)	I ask, ask for
mitto, -ere, misi (3)	I send	Roma, -ae f.	Rome
moneo, -ere, monui (2)	I warn	Romanus, -a, -um	Roman
moveo, -ere, movi (2)	I move		
mox	soon	sacer, sacra, sacrum	holy, sacred
multus, -a, -um	much, many	saepe	often
murus, -i m.	wall	saevus, -a, -um	savage
		sagitta, -ae f.	arrow
nauta, -ae m.	sailor	scribo , -ere, scripsi (3)	I write
navigo (1)	I sail	scrips-	(perf. of *scribo*)
-ne?	(indicates a question)	scutum, -i n.	shield
neco (1)	I kill	sed	but
non	not	semper	always
nos	we	septem	seven
noster, -tra, -trum	our	servus, -i m.	slave
notus, -a, -um	well known	sex	six
novem	nine	sic	thus, in this way
numquam	never	silva, -ae f.	wood, forest

socius, -i m.	ally, comrade
specto (1)	I look at, watch
statim	immediately
stet-	(perf. of *sto*)
sto, stare, steti (1)	I stand
subito	suddenly
sum, esse, fui (irreg.)	I am
supero (1)	I overcome, beat
suus, -a, -um	his/her/their own
tamen	however
tandem	finally, at last
templum, -i n.	temple
teneo, -ere, tenui (2)	I hold
terra, -ae f.	land, ground
terreo, -ere, terrui (2)	I frighten
timeo, -ere, timui (2)	I fear
trans + acc.	across
tres	three
Troia, -ae f.	Troy
Troianus, -a, -um	Trojan
tu	you (sg.)
turba, -ae f.	crowd

tutus, -a, -um	safe
tuus, -a, -um	your (sg.)
ubi	when
ubi?	where?
unda, -ae f.	wave
unus	one
validus, -a, -um	strong
venio, -ire, veni (4)	I come
ventus, -i m.	wind
verbum, -i n.	word
vester, -tra, -trum	your (pl.)
via, -ae f.	road, street, way
video, -ere, vidi (2)	I see
villa, -ae f.	villa, house
vinum, -i n.	wine
vir, viri m.	man
voco (1)	I call
vos	you (pl.)
vox, vocis f.	voice
vulnero (1)	I wound
vulnus, vulneris n.	wound